Trainer's Bonanza

Over 1000 Fabulous Tips & Tools

Eric Jensen

Trainer's Bonanza
Over 1000 Fabulous Tips & Tools

© 1998 Eric Jensen

Cover design and layout by Tracy Sciacca
Editing by Karen Markowitz

Printed in the United States of America
Published by The Brain Store, Inc.
San Diego, CA, USA

ISBN #1-890460-03-6

For additional copies, or bulk discounts,
contact: The Brain Store
4202 Sorrento Valley Blvd. #B
San Diego, CA 92121 USA
e-mail: edubrain@connectnet.com
(619) 546-7555 phone
(619) 546-7560 fax

Dedicated to my wife Diane
for her incalculable love and support

5 Ways to Get the Most Out of This Book

1 Highlight the Key Ideas

- ◆ Use colored post-it-note flags.
- ◆ Dog-ear the pages you like the most.
- ◆ Use a fluorescent highlighter.

2 Create Visual Tools or Mind Maps

On a large sheet of paper, map out the key ideas graphically. Start with the topic in the center, and add branches like a tree to represent secondary topics. Color in key ideas, and personalize it with simple illustrations.

3 Use Index Cards

- ◆ Using colored index cards, color code ideas and topics for easy organization.
- ◆ Write "Today's Idea" at the top of each card and then include one idea or strategy per card.
- ◆ Bring the cards with you to your presentations and use ideas as needed.
- ◆ Keep the card with "today's idea" on the top of the rubber-banded stack.
- ◆ On the flip side of the card, record results and suggestions for the next time.

4 Use Poster Paper

- ◆ Take three ideas and write them out on a sheet of flip chart paper.
- ◆ Post them at the back of the room at your next presentation.
- ◆ The participants will most likely never see your "cheat sheet," but it's okay if they do. It's additional reinforcement.

5 Use Partners

- ◆ With a partner, colleague or presenting buddy, discuss your ideas before and after you try them.
- ◆ Troubleshoot the idea and brainstorm what would make it better.
- ◆ Debrief it afterwards.

Table of Contents

118 Ideas: Planning the Content

22 Powerful Research Questions to Ask About Your Audience.....................1
5 Principles for Designing Presentations.........................2
10 Questions to Ask Before You Plan Your Talk.........................3
7 Deadly Presenter Mistakes.........................4
21 Ways to Improve Formal Presentations.........................6
5 Steps to Better Inductive Learning.........................7
7 Smart Chunks to a Better Seminar Format.........................8
6 Steps to Better Deductive Learning.........................10
12 Strategies to Include in Your Planning Process.........................11
14 Smart Handout Formatting Ideas.........................12
9 Essential Content Handouts for Every Presentation.....................13

85 Ideas: Preparing Yourself

17 Tips to Lower Presenter's Stress.........................16
16 Clothing and Dress Reminders.........................17
8 Ways to Prompt Your Presentation.........................18
23 Strategies to Reduce the Butterflies.........................19
21 Highly Effective Trainer Supplies.........................20

193 Ideas: Adding Variety and Interest

10 Best Uses of Technology.........................22
12 Tips for Computer Graphics.........................24
13 Tips for Preparing Audience-Friendly Transparencies.........................25
19 Best Presenting Props.........................27
27 Most Energizing Music Selections.........................28
17 Most Relaxing Music Selections.........................29
4 Best Music Selections for Priming the Brain.........................30
33 Low Energy Music Suggestions - Situation Specific.........................31
28 High Energy Music Suggestions - Situation Specific.........................33
7 Ideas for Seating Variety.........................34
13 Suggestions for Using Overhead Transparency Projectors.........................35
10 Hot Tips for Flip Charts and White Boards.........................36

77 Ideas: Insurance Policies

7   Things You Must Learn About Your Audience.................................39
11 Ways to Better Prepare Your Audience..40
10 Problems Waiting to Happen...41
19 Item "To Do" List for Sponsors..42
30 Ways to Manage the Micro- Details..44

46 Ideas: Starting Off on the Right Foot

6   Openers to Avoid...47
7   Great Ways to Get Started..48
5   Things to Say in the First 30 Seconds...49
6   Rules for Positive Openings..50
9   Instant Icebreakers...51
8   Ways to Warm a Chilly Climate..53
5   Audience De-stressors...54

75 Ideas: Building Good Relationships

15 Audience Relationship-Builders..56
25 Ways to Achieve Credibility..57
25 Habits That Spell Professionalism...58
10 Personal Rapport-Builders...60

160 Ideas: Insuring Optimal Learning

11 Ways to Enhance the Learning Process..63
14 Ideas for Enhanced Processing Time...64
54 Ways to Deepen Learning..65
14 Active Processing Strategies...67
15 Thinking Activities..68
13 Mind Mapping Techniques...69
20 Ways to Provide More Feedback...70
12 Strategies to Enhance Verification..71
7   Ways to Celebrate the Learning...72

72 Ideas: Facilitating Great Audience Interactions

9   Most Common Threats to Avoid..74
11 Tips for Creating a Safe Climate...75
8   Deadly Audience Mistakes to Avoid..76
4   Ways to Answer Tough Questions and Preserve Credibility.............77
7   Non-Verbal Rapport-Building Strategies......................................78

14 Tools for Quick Rapport-Building..79

13 First Aid Tips for Heckled Presenters......................................80

6   Questioning Strategies...81

149 Ideas: Engaging the Learner

26 Ways to Motivate Learners...83

19 Ways to Get Attention..84

14 Ways to Engage Emotions...85

21 Quickie Tips for Getting Audience Cooperation.......................86

14 Fun Group Bonding Rituals..87

14 More Wild Attention Getters...88

5   Ideas for Physical Participation..89

7   Ideas for Greater Conversational Participation.......................90

18 Quick Ways to Form Partnerships..92

11 Ways to Form Instant Groups...94

25 Ideas: Sharpening Your Communications

12 Key Nonverbal Signals..97

5   Smart Things to Do With Your Hands......................................98

8   Easy Steps for Providing Effective Instructions.....................99

66 Ideas: Quickie Energizers and State Changers

7   Secrets for an Energized Audience...101

50 State Change Suggestions...103

9   Active Stretch Breaks Ideas...104

54 Ideas: Learning Transfer

16 Ways to Insure Participants Remember....................................106

24 Useful Strategies for Long-term Retention...............................107

14 Ideas That Nearly Guarantee Transfer of Learning...............108

67 Ideas: Combining Fun With Learning

13 Tips for Better Activities...110

6   Highly Effective Activity Signals..111

7   Limited Space Activities..112

7   Open Space Activities...114

6   Discussion Activities..116

5   Extra-Loud Activities...117

5   Physically Charged Team Activities...118

18 Team Affirmations..119

50 Ideas: Closing Your Presentation

8   Keys to Perfect Closings...121
14 Ways to Elicit a Feeling of Movement.......................................122
13 Strategies to Insure Meaning and Value...................................123
15 Tips to Elicit a Feeling of Completion......................................124

37 Ideas: Trainer Goodies

7   Cases When You Should Turn Down Work..............................126
7   Tips for Deciding How Much to Charge....................................127
12 Best Trainer Books and Conferences..128
11 Best Trainer Resources for Body and Brain.............................129

About the Author...130
Notes, Thoughts, and Reader Feedback..131

Trainer's Bonanza

Over 1000 Fabulous Tips & Tools

118 Ideas:
Planning the Content

22 Powerful Research Questions to Ask About Your Audience

The best way to insure your presentation will meet the needs of your audience is to find out about them. The following questions will give you a framework for this important aspect of your presentation:

◆ What will the mindset of the learners or audience likely be?
◆ What do the learners already know?
◆ Will your participants' place of employment likely support your ideas?
◆ Has your topic been "set up well" or has it been "contaminated?"
◆ What does the audience bring to the topic?
◆ What is the prime reason the learners are there?
◆ What do members of the audience have in common with each other?
◆ What is the age and gender breakdown of the audience?
◆ What are the participants' expectations of quality?
◆ Who will be your inside contacts?
◆ Did your audience volunteer or is attendance required?
◆ Will lunch be provided in house or will they go out for it?
◆ What is the average experience of your audience members?
◆ What are the likely biases, the beliefs and prejudices of your audience?
◆ What will the likely circumstances be?
◆ How much time is allotted for your presentation?
◆ Can you go a few minutes over the allotted time if you need to?
◆ What is the common vocabulary or slang you ought to avoid?
◆ What resources do you have available?
◆ Is anyone else speaking before you? Who? and What is their topic?
◆ When can you get into the room to set up?
◆ What are the logistics of location, parking, traffic, time frames?

 The more questions you ask and the better the quality of questions you ask, the greater the likelihood you'll discover what you really need to know for success.

5 Principles for Designing Presentations

1 Climate Before Content

Unless your participants feel good in the learning environment, learning will either be impaired or contaminated. Specifically, remove any and all forms of threat and any excessive stressors. Help learners feel valued, cared about, included and special. Insure everything in the environment from plants to procedures has a positive purpose and speaks to the dignity of the learner and the joy of learning.

2 Each Learner is Unique

Do you provide an experience first and then label it? Or do you label an experience first and then experience it? Do you use the 4-MAT learning styles model, Dunn and Dunn, Herrmann's or that of Gregorc? What about visual, auditory and kinesthetic modalities or multiple intelligences? Every one of these ways will work—for some learners. The key is to provide a wide variety of learning choices.

3 Emotions Drive the Process

It is emotions, not logic, that drive our attention, meaning-making and memory. This suggests the importance of eliciting curiosity, suspense, humor, excitement, joy, and laughter. Each participant's efforts should be acknowledged and learning should be celebrated each and every day.

4 Orchestrate Models and Maps

Models give us our procedures, options, processes and pathways for long-term success. Individual content may be interesting to some and may translate to good scores on a test. But human understanding is dependent on content maps that lay out the territory. These are the wider patterns of learning, not the isolated facts. Make sure your participants leave with the experiences, knowledge and skills that assist them in building appropriate maps and models. These are the lifelong gifts that make your presentation worthwhile.

5 All Learning is State Dependent

We all have highs and lows, moments of anticipation, frustration, hope, apathy, hunger, and hundreds of other states. Each state mediates and influences the invitation and meaning of learning. As the leader, make it your responsibility to elicit productive states for learning every time. When it's appropriate, teach learners how to manage their own states so they're empowered to take care of themselves.

10 Questions to Ask Before You Plan Your Talk

1 What events should you avoid bringing up?

2 Are there names of previous presenters you should use or avoid?

3 How many years of experience does your average attendee have?

4 What are their likely fears and prejudices?

5 What common vocabulary or slang should you avoid?

6 What will the mindset of the audience likely be?

7 What do your learners already know?

8 What happened on their last training or retreat?

9 Is there anyone that the audience respects that you can refer to?

10 Is there anyone speaking prior to your presentation? What are they likely to say? How might they impact your talk?

7 Deadly Presenter Mistakes

1 Too Much Information

It is better to limit yourself and the audience to less, but do a better job of it. First brainstorm ideas, then focus on a few keywords and ideas. Turn those into overheads. You ought to be able to summarize your whole talk on an overhead transparency or slide in just a few words. In a one hour talk, three key points is perfect; never more than five.

2 Talking Only About Content Not People

Even in the most technical presentations, the audience enjoys hearing the human side of a story. Talk about your own excitements, frustrations, hopes and dreams. Bring in colleagues or your spouse. Make it a humane presentation about content, not a technical presentation about details.

3 Treating Audience Members With Disinterest

Ask about the make-up of the audience in advance to gain any insights as to their special needs and interests. Address them by profession if you can. Use examples that match their experiences. Learn what makes the group and individuals within it unique.

4 Inadequate Preparation

Before your talk, go through all of your materials and ask yourself if they are truly up to date; if they reflect the interests of the audience; and if they are first class. If they don't meet the highest standards, it's time for an update.

5 Lack of Attention to the Opening

Your audience will make up their mind in the first thirty seconds about whether you're worth listening to or not. Make sure you are clear, crisp, enthusiastic and approachable.

6 Too Technical or Full of Jargon

Make sure that you use (even in technical presentations) metaphors, analogies and examples that make even the most complex subjects more accessible. As an example, one neuroscientist calls the cellular bonding between peptide messengers and receptor sites "molecular sex." This gets attention and says it all.

7 Lack of Interaction With the Audience

Make eye contact. Be enthusiastic. Vary the pace. Get out from behind the lectern often. Use gestures. Use humor. Involve the audience by asking for their opinion. Do a survey or ask if a particular event has happened to them. Get them involved and they'll remember your presentation better. Give them your expectations about question asking at the very start of the presentation.

Can you recall a presentation you've attended that was invaluable? What do you think made it so good?

21 Ways to Improve Formal Presentations

- Get excited over the material; role model joy!
- Bring something special and relevant: book, article, music, or prop.
- Put a visual overview up on board, flipchart, or overhead projector.
- Do something slightly different: new seating, music, posters on walls, etc.
- Always open with a positive greeting, excitement and appreciation.
- Get attention with a special quote, mystery question, an object, a music lead off, or with an unusual story, case problem or overhead transparency.
- Answer the question that every participant is surely asking: "What's in it for me?"
- Read the the state of the audience and stay in touch with it.
- Offer headline-style objectives or today's menu at the onset.
- Offer pre- and post-view attractions and TUF (your *talk's uniqueness factor*).
- Never read your talk word-for-word. Use key phrases and key words and key topics and speak from these.
- Use visual aids as your prompts or cues. This includes flip charts, white boards, overhead transparencies or computer-based projection systems.
- Be excited about what you do; implore learners to write down something every few minutes as you talk; make it relevant!
- Lecture a maximum of 12 to 20 consecutive minutes, then stop to avoid saturation! Have learners stretch, stand, reflect, and discuss things to break up the lecture format.
- If you lose your place or get stuck, give everyone a quick stand and stretch break. This will give you some time to get back on track.
- Do an experiment with the audience.
- Ask questions like, "Who has had this happen?"
- Conduct quick audience surveys by asking for a show of hands.
- Review key points on an overhead transparency.
- Have learners share or review what they have learned with a partner.
- Always end on a "high note"— memorable story, interesting statistic, or catchy slogan.

Steps to Better Inductive Learning

The following formats provide effective ways to introduce new material to your audience. Each format is generally just a micro-sequence of your presentation, rather than encompassing it entirely. If you are unsure how to present your material, these formats may be helpful:

INDUCTIVE:

Specific to General - the What, How, Why of It!

1 Pre-exposure to the Topic

Mention what the group will be doing and why. Discuss time-frames and schedules.

2 Hands-on, Real-life Experiences

These include: field trips, simulations, learning on the job, games, etc.

3 Debrief With a Partner

Share personal experiences. It could be "find a partner" or "work in your team."

4 Whole Group Discussion

Facilitate discussion that is linked to your topic. Find out what others talked about, elicit ideas, and tie in research or things you forgot to mention.

5 Personal Applications and Goal-Setting

Have participants decide which strategies they want to personally commit to using; or what they want to get out of the training.

7 Smart Chunks to a Better Seminar Format

1 Preparation
- Do research on the audience.
- Prepare them for the material.
- Create an environment of immersion.

2 Globalization - the "Why"
- Pre-expose all content. Create expectation.
- Build rapport. Set up systems for success.
- Establish context and relevance.
- Show the benefits and value.
- Give the classic "big picture."

3 Initiation - the "What"
- Get started with hands-on action.
- Use discovery learning or simulations.
- Use deadlines, teams, partners or a project.

4 Elaboration - the "How"
- Provide understanding to the deeper questions.
- Get details handled, do problem-solving.
- Offer explanations, forecasting, and insights.

5 Incubation - the "Nonconscious"
- Provide reflection time.
- Provide processing time or day off.
- Provide breaks often.

6 Verification - the "Knowing That I Know It"

- ◆ Demonstrate learning.
- ◆ Conduct role-plays or performances.
- ◆ Do hands-on activities.
- ◆ Plan the assessment.
- ◆ Do mind-mapping.
- ◆ Conduct debates.
- ◆ Ask "what if" questions.

7 Celebration - the Feeling of Success

- ◆ See, hear, and share ideas.
- ◆ Provide acknowledgments.
- ◆ Highlight results.
- ◆ Provide mini parties or rituals.

Are you planning a presentation? How will you accomplish each of the seven smart chunks above?

6 Steps to Better Deductive Learning

DEDUCTIVE:
General to Specific - the What, Why, How of It!

1 Pre-exposure to the Topic

Mention what the group will be doing and why. Share time frames and schedule for the whole training.

2 Relevancy

Use personal experiences. Associate with both professional experiences (first) and personal experiences (second). For example, ask, "How many of you have had this happen to you.....?"

3 Links to Brain Research

Present the science side. Give names, locations, history, references, and results.

4 Participants Generate Applications of the Research

This is best done within the context of the team or in a temporary group.

5 Sharing

Do this with partners, jigsaw or with group discussion. Whatever grouping you use, regroup for fresh, different ideas the next time.

6 Personal Decision

Create and share the "next step." Participants narrow options and choose the most viable ones for themselves; then share them with the rest of their group.

12 Strategies to Include in Your Planning Process

◆ **Pre-expose the learners to the topic -** (it can be done hours, days and weeks in advance: this helps the brain build better conceptual maps).

◆ **Offer learning-to-learn skills.**

◆ **Present brain nutrition and offer coping, self-esteem and life skills.**

◆ **Create a strong immersion learning environment; make it interesting!**

◆ **Reinforce your own credibility and prestige.**

◆ **Plan the best time of day for learning each item based on brain cycles and bio-rhythms.**

◆ **Discover participants' interests and backgrounds.**

◆ **Make sure your environment has many colorful posters.**

◆ **Provide brain "wake-ups"** (cross-laterals or relax-stretching).

◆ **State strong positive expectations; allow learners to voice theirs as well and to set their own goals for the training.**

◆ **Create relationships; build strong positive rapport.**

◆ **Read audience states and make any adjustments before beginning.**

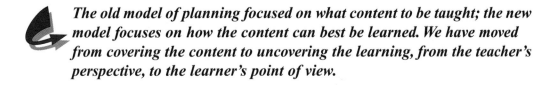

The old model of planning focused on what content to be taught; the new model focuses on how the content can best be learned. We have moved from covering the content to uncovering the learning, from the teacher's perspective, to the learner's point of view.

Smart Handout Formatting Ideas

◆ Use fewer, rather than more pages.

◆ Include references at the back.

◆ Give the handouts at the very beginning, when they enter or register. Don't hold handouts until the end as this is irritating to many participants and insulting to others.

◆ Make them interactive—leave blank spaces to fill in from the presentation material.

◆ Print on only one side of the page—leave the other side for notes.

◆ Include a one-page summary of your presentation.

◆ Avoid the details; give only key ideas.

◆ Use just enough graphics to keep attention.

◆ Number the pages so the audience can follow along easily.

◆ Tell the audience up front if the pages are reproducible.

◆ Make sure your name and number are on several pages.

◆ Provide references for your quotes and factual statements.

◆ Give additional resources for follow-up.

◆ Print up extras— make enough for the number attendees, plus 10 to 30 percent more.

Essential Content Handouts for Every Presentation

1 The Cover Page

On the cover page have the title of the presentation, your name, a place for their name and an icon or graphic that summarizes the topic of the presentation. Give your presentation a strong title. Instead of "Fundamentals of Customer Service," say "How to Turn Your Customers into Raving Fans in 7 Easy Steps." Then follow through on your promise in the course.

2 The Ground Rules Page

This page sets the frame work for a positive climate. I call it the "How to make this a terrific success" page. This is most appropriate for seminars and workshops one day in length or longer.

3 The Hook Page

This is a page that helps the audience see the relevance of your topic. This page is most appropriate for audiences who were required to come to your presentation.

4 The Goals Page

For workshops of a day or longer, it makes sense for participants to set goals. Your goal page should not only ask for goals, but ask them why they want to accomplish them.

5 The Summary Page

There ought to be a single page that summarizes your entire presentation.

6 The Content Pages

This may take from five to fifty pages depending on the length of the workshop, the need for handouts, and the type of information needed by the audience. Most presenters use about 10 to 20 pages a day.

7 The Note Pages

Participants can use the backside of other printed pages for notes. This saves trees and allows the participants to make notes directly opposite the material that they're referencing.

8 The Additional Resources Page

Many participants enjoy knowing where they can get more information on your topic. Be sure to list:

- ◆ lay-person books
- ◆ technical books
- ◆ videos available
- ◆ testimonials of graduates
- ◆ other workshops and seminars
- ◆ key people in your field
- ◆ movies or videos to rent
- ◆ products to purchase
- ◆ best conferences to attend
- ◆ e-mail or INTERNET contacts and WEB sites

9 The Evaluation/Feedback Page

This is certainly one of the most important parts of the handouts. You'll have to experiment until you get the quality and quantity of feedback that's useful for you.

 The use of color in your handouts creates reactions and interest. Whether consciously or subconsciously, the opportunity to attract your audience's attention ought never be missed.

85 Ideas: Preparing Yourself

Tips on How to Lower Presentation Stress

- Workout daily to keep your stress response system in top form.

- Drink plenty of water. Five to eight glasses per day is recommended.

- Eat energy bars for mid-morning and mid-afternoon pick-me-ups.

- Practice yoga. Yoga can reduce stress to both your mind and body; and it can be done anywhere and requires no special clothing or equipment.

- Eat breakfast. If you want to be at your sharpest, eat more proteins than carbohydrates; and eat the proteins first. For breakfast, you might have juice, fruit, eggs, and ham or cottage cheese.

- Eat lunch. Have a tuna or chicken salad with lots of vegies.

- Visualize success. Instead of worrying, visualize how well you'll do. This is a form of mental practice and goal-setting.

- Redirect your self-talk. Every time you start to give yourself a negative message, stop. Take a deep breath and say to yourself, "I can do a great job. I am prepared. I can't control how the audience will respond, but I can control how I respond. I will be relaxed and confident. I will be in control of myself."

- Wake up your eyes. Put your palms over your eyebrows and eyes and press in gently. Let your eyes relax before removing your hands.

- Stretch your face. Make as many different faces as you can. Scrunch it up and make it as small as you can. Then, open it up as wide as you can. Stretch your face muscles again, your mouth and eyes. Let them relax.

- Shake out your hands to increase circulation. Hold them high and shake again.

- Give yourself a brief massage on your shoulders and neck. Do neck rolls.

- Take a deep breath. Exhale slowly. Repeat, and let your shoulders relax.

- Do some cross-laterals. Touch opposite knees, opposite elbows, opposite shoulder blades and opposite knees. Take a slow, deep breath again. Stretch your shoulders back slowly.

- Do some jumping-jacks, sit-ups, stair-stepping, or walking.

- Repeat your affirming self-talk. Provide positive programming.

- Stand up straight. Feel confident, hold your head high, and smile deeply.

Clothing and Dress Reminders

- Generally, dress "beyond" your audience, but be certain that it is appropriate for the occasion.

- For men, suits are best for formal presentations. A white shirt and dark tie is still the protocol (take a look at members of Congress!)

- For men, a sport coat and slacks is still the norm for informal groups.

- More shirt colors are becoming accepted for business, semi-formal and casual wear. Don't forget how color can make a statement.

- In New England, and in the South and upper Midwest, you'll find more white shirts and suits than in the West.

- Make sure your belt and shoes match and are of top quality.

- For both genders, darker colors enhance credibility.

- If you know that you already have high credibility with your audience, you can wear lighter, more casual clothes.

- For women, dresses or skirt suits are considered the norm for business wear.

- Pantsuits are also gaining wide acceptance as professional wear for women.

- Accessories should add to and not distract from your professional image.

- Carry a briefcase or keep your purse subtle and low key.

- Women tend to be judged quickly by their appearance - especially hair style, make-up, and the "loudness" of dress.

- Avoid wearing distracting colors or noisy jewelry.

- If you're wearing something unusual that will likely draw the audience's attention, simply mention it early on in your presentation so that curiosity about it is decreased.

- For both genders, sensible shoes and clothing that you feel comfortable wearing and allows for ease of movement is of paramount importance.

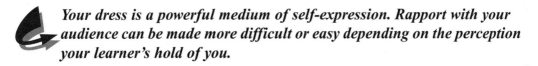

Your dress is a powerful medium of self-expression. Rapport with your audience can be made more difficult or easy depending on the perception your learner's hold of you.

8 Ways to Prompt Your Presentation

Notes and prompts are not inherently bad to use. In fact, many of the very best presenters in the world use them. The key is to use notes and prompts effectively. Here are eight ways to do that:

1 Index Cards

Create a generalized outline listing the key parts of your presentation and record it on index cards.

2 3-Ring Binder

Include pertinent information on notebook paper which can be rearranged in a 3-ring binder and leafed through as you talk.

3 Mind-Maps

These can be recorded on index cards, in a binder, or posted.

4 Props

Use only props that relate to the specific topic you are covering. One comedian has his entire routine choreographed with props.

5 Transparencies

These highly visual cue cards are easy to develop, use, see by your audience, and store for later use.

6 Flip Charts

Write out your key points on a large sheet of flip chart or poster paper. Post at the back of the room or use them as a guide as you flip through your presentation.

7 Computer

Use your laptop or other computer to guide your talk. A visual presentation can be prepared on the computer and connected to a unit that projects the image onto the wall or movie screen. Or, you can use your monitor for your own reference only.

8 Audience Questions

Have the audience submit questions in advance and you pre-select the ones you would like to answer.

23 Strategies to Reduce the "Butterflies"

- Practice!
- Work with similar groups prior to the "big talk." This helps you try out statements, jokes, comments, opinions and subject content that might be susceptible to audience disapproval.
- Drop unpopular points or comments before it really counts.
- Experiment with your material on a small volunteer audience out of town.
- Try out small chunks if you can't get a chance to do the whole thing.
- Get feedback on trial presentations so you know what to change.
- Make up a list of key points on poster paper and post them up high in the back of the room where you'll be presenting.
- Use a series of props with either the key words on them, or simply let the props trigger the content.
- Create a memory peg system so each part of your talk is "linked up" to a cue. For example, if your talk is about customer service, you might link the five key topics to parts of the body. The head is for thinking through your response, the heart for empathizing with the customer, etc.
- Practice with your prompts and props to make sure that you've got the routine down.
- Rehearse your talk and have it tape recorded or videotaped so you can modify what you don't like and emphasize what you do.
- Rehearse the material under a bit of stress. If you match your likely state for the real thing, you will insure that the knowledge and skills you've prepared will be available when needed.
- Mentally walk through your presentation.
- Memorize your index cards (or mind map).
- Rehearse your key gestures.
- Practice in front of the mirror.
- Study other successful speakers.
- Learn a good joke that your audience will surely love.
- Visualize success.
- Exercise or do a physical activity that has nothing to do with your presentation.
- Test and quiz yourself. When you have a few moments, write out the opening one minute of your presentation.
- Sit where the audience will be sitting. Get a feel for their perspective.
- Relax, breathe deeply.

21 Highly Effective Trainer Supplies

Every presenter or trainer carries a supply bag or "goodie box." The contents vary dramatically because of the type of message you have, your audience, and the length of your typical presentation. Some important items that all presenters need to be prepared include:

◆ **Batteries** (spares for equipment you use)
◆ **Blank transparencies**
◆ **Blu-tak** (sticky putty for posters)
◆ **Box-cutter/penknife**
◆ **CD/cassette player**
◆ **Computer**
◆ **Course transparencies**
◆ **Electronic/laser pointer**
◆ **Extension cord**
◆ **Flip chart paper** (Post-It 3M easel pads are great)
◆ **Legal pad for notes**
◆ **Microphone system**
◆ **Multiple outlets/surge control**
◆ **Pens, overhead pens, markers**
◆ **Post-it notes** (small and big)
◆ **Products/books to show and demonstrate**
◆ **Projection system**
◆ **Props for demo or toss-around**
◆ **Set of handout masters in case workbook is lost or you need more**
◆ **Tape** (masking, duct, transparent)
◆ **Whistle, noisemaker, attention-getter**

193 Ideas:

Adding Variety & Interest

10 Best Uses of Technology

1 Computers

It is easy to transmit data directly from your computer to a large screen. The software to facilitate this function is improving all the time. The color and graphics capabilities are too good to pass up. Professionally formatted visuals is now the Industry standard.

2 Ionizers

These are the small units which charge the air with negative ions. More and more businesses are using them. They can increase alertness and learning. How much of a difference do they make? Fresh air is best, but if you can't get it, these are second best. They cost from $100 to $400.

3 Overheads

The days of traditional transparencies are numbered. Though they provide visuals at a low initial cost, audiences are becoming more sophisticated and their expectations are higher.

4 Pointers

The red laser pointers, though expensive, are no longer a luxury. If you don't have one, get one. And be sure to bring a spare set of batteries or a spare pointer with you to presentations or trainings.

5 Projection Systems

Instead of a TV system with a small screen, many presenters use the huge-screen projection systems. They usually work with a high-intensity overhead projector to deliver a huge picture.

6 Software

The most commonly used software programs are PowerPoint, Freelance Graphics or Harvard Graphics.

7 Sound Systems

If the facility does not have a good quality sound system, either bring your own or rent one from a local audio/visual company. Today, you can purchase a system that will allow you to custom-record your own tunes or effects on a CD. While, perhaps, a bit expensive, the convenience of having a "customer" training CD is hard to beat.

8 Transparencies

If you are going to use them, make them first class. Many printers can now print in bold clean colors.

9 Variable Lighting

Make use of the selective lighting panels to insure that the room is light (and dark) where you need it to be.

10 Video

Never show more than 10 to 15 minutes of a video at a time—the audience will go into a "trance-state." Show only what you're willing to invest time in debriefing.

What equipment will you need for your presentation?

Tips for Computer Graphics

- Be bold! Do catchy, alluring, entertaining, relevant, attention-getting graphics. But make sure they are directly related to the topic of your presentation.

- Make a catchy presentation title. Instead of "Applications of Recent Brain Research," use, "Brain-Smart Trainings that Boost Learning by 50%."

- Start with the big picture. Create graphics that summarize what you're going to present and use them as an overview. They can be in the form of a mind map, a list of key items or a single graphic. Make sure everyone knows where you're going before you start.

- Use sufficient margins. Use a small margin at the top of the frame, larger one at the bottom. Better to go wider than longer.

- Use bar graphs to show increases or comparisons. Color code the bars for maximum contrast and interest.

- Use font types sparingly in each piece you design. In other words, if you start a piece using Helvetica, don't also incorporate Times and Palatino. Use the largest font size for the most important points; and then prioritize down from there with respectively smaller font sizes. Match fonts to the tone, style and expectations of your presentation and target audience.

- Use an area chart to show volume. An area chart is a better indicator of how much of something is involved.

- Use large type on computer graphics. Use about five lines or fewer. Phrases are better than complete sentences. Upper-lower case is easier to read than all caps.

- Use flowcharts to show processes. Even the most complex processes need simple, understandable steps. If needed, use several in a sequence.

- End Your presentation with a catchy graphic. Use the last thought, call to action, or "Thank You" in conjunction with the graphic. This is your opportunity to make a final lasting impression.

- Always double-check and have someone else proofread your material before finalizing it. Use your computer's spell check.

- Do a complete run through of your presentation using all of your graphics before doing the real thing.

13 Tips for Preparing Audience-Friendly Transparencies

1 Big

Make your letters and words big and easy to read.

2 Test Ideas

Place the overhead transparency projector (OHT) on the floor. If you can read it while standing, it's okay.

3 Color

Use vibrant colors—red, blue and green, but avoid making them too dark. Use moderate saturation to make it easy on the eyes. Use permanent markers, not water based; and shade the back of overhead to add quick color. If you're in a bind and need to create a color transparency in a hurry, try this. Print it in black and white and use a permanent market (colored one) on the back of the transparency. The water-based markers won't do; they have to be the permanent ones. You can add colorful touches, fill in spaces, or add borders that give it a quick "dress up" for a sophisticated audience.

4 Themes

Use color for a reason, such as to differentiate between points. Avoid random splashes of color. Instead, color code themes, ideas or build ups.

5 Use Graphics

Pictures convey a thousand words. Keep them clear and tasteful.

6 Highlight Key Ideas Only

Transparencies ought to convey only your major ideas. Use them to prompt your talk, not to take its place.

7 Use Five or Fewer Ideas Per Transparency

The fewer the key ideas you present in each transparency, the more likely it will be remembered. In most cases, use just one key idea per transparency unless you're giving a list or summary.

8 Combine

Use both upper and lower case letters. All caps is hard to read. Use highlights, underlines, bolds or all caps sparingly. Too many highlights defeat their purpose.

9 Space

Use only the top 70 percent of the transparency. The space below this point is awkward to center on the screen.

10 Build

If your idea is complex, build into it with several transparencies that start general and get progressively more specific. Label, number or identify key points on each transparency.

11 Re-write

Never copy a written page out of a book and use it as is—always re-do it to make it more readable, applicable to your unique situation, and concise.

12 Use Icons and Simple Illustrations

Avoid complicated drawings or complex pictures.

13 Post-It Notes

Put post-its on the far edges or the bottom of a transparency to label them for easy retrieval and reorganization.

Best Presenting Props

About 90 percent of all presentations can be enhanced by the use of a prop. If you think your presentation falls into the rare 10 percent category that can't benefit from props, watch television. This visual medium provides constant sources of sight gags that presenters can benefit from using. The following list provides some ideas:

◆ **Party noisemakers**

◆ **Hats** (chef's, Sherlock Holmes, baseball, magician's hard hat, etc.)

◆ **Oversized pair of glasses**

◆ **Magic show props like a magic wand**

◆ **Stuffed animals**

◆ **Celebrity masks** (best time to get them is Halloween)

◆ **Movie director's snap-boards** "Take one, take two, etc."

◆ **Artificial body parts** (hands, legs, wigs, etc.)

◆ **Inflatables** (beach balls, toys, chairs, etc.)

◆ **Rubber or plastic brains**

◆ **Hand puppets**

◆ **Balls of all sizes** (Koosh, rubber, beach, etc.)

◆ **An empty picture frame** (to put a frame around an activity)

◆ **A rubber chicken** (or other animal)

◆ **Cardboard models of the concept you are talking about**

◆ **Monster masks**

◆ **"Groucho" noses**

◆ **A squirt gun**

◆ **A towel** (if need be, you can always "throw in the towel")

 There's something whimsical, safe, and engaging about props; and it's not just the presenter who can us them. Keep a large prop box for occasions where you want to increase novelty, interest, and engage emotions in learners as well.

27 Highly Energetic Music Selections

- *C'Mon N' Ride It* by Quad City D.J.s
- *Hooked on Classics*
- *A Deeper Love* by Aretha Franklin
- *Macarena* by Los Del Mar
- *Be My Lover* by La Bouche
- *Hawaii Five-O* theme
- *I Like to Move It* by Reel 2 Reel
- *Miami Vice* theme by Jan Hammer
- *Boom Boom Boom* by Outhere Brothers
- Themes from *Star Wars*
- *Raiders of the Lost Ark* theme
- *Another Night* by Real McCoy
- *O-Bla-Di-O-Bla-Da* by the Beatles
- *The Big Bang* (Drums!) by Ellipsis Arts 3400
- *Where Do You Go* by No Mercy
- *The Best of Chic: Dance, Dance, Dance* by Chic (Techno-pop)
- Get Collections of Dance Party CDs
- *Tell it To My Heart* by Taylor Dayne
- Steelbands of Trinidad and Tobago
- *Heart of Steel* by Flying Fish
- *Mission Impossible* theme
- *This is Your Night* by Amber
- *Rocky* theme
- *Total Eclipse of the Heart* by Nicki French
- *Chariots of Fire* by Vangelis,
- *Eye of the Tiger* by Survivor
- *Break on Through* by the Doors

Most Relaxing Music Selections

Music by the following artists are a safe bet to help relax your audience:

- David Arkenstone
- Ayman
- Keola Beamer
- Jim Chappell
- Kenny G
- Adam Geiger
- Nicholas Gunn
- Steven Halpern
- Georgia Kelly
- Kitaro
- Daniel Kobialka
- Mars Lasar
- Tony O'Connor
- Paul Speer and David Lanz
- Hillary Stagg
- George Winston
- Zamfir

Also, the collections and anthologies are excellent. You may also want to explore: ◆ Chrysalis by 2002 ◆ Rain Forest music ◆ Bird Symphony ◆ The National Park Series

Commonly used Baroque selections are:
◆ "Four Seasons" by Vivaldi ◆ "Brandenburg Concertos" by Bach ◆ "Water Music" by Handel. Other Baroque artists include ◆ Bach ◆ Corelli ◆ Tartini ◆ Vivaldi ◆ Albinoni ◆ Handel ◆ Fausch and Pachelbel.

When selecting these (often found in the "bargain bins"), make sure most of the compositions are played in the major (upbeat) key and done by a full orchestra (not one or two violins).

Best Music Selections for Priming the Brain

Some music is better for arousal (i.e., theme from *Rocky*). Yet you can also prepare your learners for better learning with specific music. We know the neural firing patterns are very similar for music appreciation and abstract spatial reasoning.

1 Sonatas for Two Pianos in D Major by Beethoven

2 Daphne et Chole Suite #2 by Maurice Ravel

3 Symphony in 3 Movements by Igor Stravinsky

4 Laya Vinyas by Trichy Sankran

Caution: Listening to this music for 10 minutes (controlled relaxation) before beginning a specific task using spatial reasoning (assembling objects, mind-mapping, jigsaw puzzles, flow charts, etc.) is valuable. This is because the rate your brain cells fire at is enhanced by particular types of music. Listening to the music, however, while working on a project causes neural competition and interference with the neural firing pattern. Time music listening, therefore, appropriately.

> *How can you use music for priming the brain in your next presentation?*

33 Low-Energy Music Suggestions

For Visualization, Relaxation, Stretching and Imagery

- Daniel Kobialka
- Georgia Kelly
- Kitaro
- George Winston
- Michael Jones
- Environmental Music: birds, flute, waterfalls

Mindset for Creativity

- *Piano Concerto #5* by Beethoven
- *Etudes* by Chopin
- *Claire de Lune* by Debussy
- *Piano Concerto #26 & 27* Mozart
- *Swan Lake* by Tchaikovsky
- *Blue Danube* by Strauss
- *Fantasia* by Disney
- *Suites for Orchestra* by Bach
- *Toy Symphonies* by Haydn
- *Musical Joke* by Mozart
- *Desert Vision* by Speer and Lanz
- *Natural States* by Lanz and Speer

Calming Music

- *Amazing Grace* (traditional spiritual song)
- *Claire de Lune* by Debussy
- *Trois Gymnopedies* by Eric Satie

Storytelling, Concert Readings and Metaphors

◆ Beethoven

◆ Mozart

◆ Haydn

◆ Wagner

◆ Dvorak

◆ Rimsky-Korsakov

Closings (for a positive ending each day)

◆ *Hi-Ho*, from *Snow White*

◆ *Tomorrow*, theme song from *Annie*

◆ Good-bye song from *Sound of Music*

◆ *What A Wonderful World* by Louis Armstrong

◆ *Happy Days* theme on Vol. #3 of TV Themes by Steven Gottleib

◆ *Happy Trails* by Roy Rogers on Vol. #1 of TV Themes by Steven Gottleib

How can you implement music for visualization, relaxation and creativity into your next presentation?

28 High-Energy Music Suggestions

Start-ups, Openings and Good Beginnings
Epic Movie Soundtracks:
- *Chariots of Fire*
- *Superman*
- *Rocky*
- *Lawrence of Arabia*
- *Born Free*
- *Dr. Zhivago*
- *Oh! What a Beautiful Morning* from Oklahoma
- *James Bond 007* soundtracks
- Ravel's *Bolero*
- *Prelude in D Major* by Bach
- *Amanda Panda* song from Saving the Wildlife by Mannheim Steamroller
- Hungarian Dances by Brahms

Special Guest Introductions
- *Fanfare for the Common Man* by Arron Copeland
- *Grand March from Aida* by Verdi
- Olympics Theme-1984 Summer Games
- *Thus Sprake Zarathrustra* (2001 Theme)
- *We Will Rock You (We are the Champions)* by Queen

Celebrations, Successes
- *9th Choral Symphony* by Beethoven
- *Celebrate* by Three Dog Night
- *Celebrate* by Madonna
- *The Creation and The Seasons* by Haydn
- *Celebration* by Kool and the Gang
- *Hallelujah Chorus* from "Messiah" by Handel

Transition Time or "High-Energy Movers"
- *Hooked on Classics* by Philadelphia Harmonics
- *1812 Overture* by Tchaikovsky
- *William Tell Overture* by Rossini
- Theme from TV's Rawhide
- *Peanuts Theme* by Giraldi or Benoit

Ideas for Seating Variety

1 Use a podium if you want to convey position, authority or pomp and circumstance (i.e. a special event). If you're going to use a podium, set it back from the group, so you can walk in front of it if you'd like. Otherwise, for a standard training or informal talk, if you can avoid using a podium, do so.

2 For group decision-making processes, arrange chairs so that group members have maximum eye contact with others involved in the process. A large circle or several smaller tables work best.

3 For a mood of formality or decision-making processes facilitated by the presenter, arrange chairs in a large "U" shape. This arrangement is best for groups with 6 to 25 members.

4 For an informational talk, lecture or demonstration, a theater style arrangement of chairs is effective. Chairs only are arranged facing the front of the room in a fanned out pattern so that the wings of the audience are angled more towards the front.

5 For encouraging teamwork, when teams have yet to be formed, start with flexible seating - chairs only. Once the teams are formed, bring in tables.

6 For teamwork in which teams have already been formed, use six foot long tables or round tables. Tables that are eight feet in length or longer are too long for effective teamwork unless they are doubled up—two across.

7 For trainings that involve a mixture of lecture, audience participation, roleplays and activities, use large areas. You can have teams work at tables, and have breakout areas for other activities.

13 Suggestions for Using Overhead Transparency Projectors

◆ Put your transparencies in clear plastic holder sheets that have holes for easy insertion into a three-ring binder. You can leave them in the holders when you use them and they will be protected. Plus the binder lets you leaf through them quickly.

◆ Duplicate key transparencies that fit into several categories.

◆ Test the projector in advance. Most overhead projectors are too dim, have poor focus ability or dirty lenses. As a result, it makes your work look bad. Ask for a specific type of projector that you know is top quality, get there early to make sure it's working well, and have a back-up plan.

◆ File transparencies by topic. Color code key topics for easy return to binder.

◆ Acid test. Put some of your "questionable" or "iffy" transparencies on the screen and sit in the back of the room. Ask yourself if they are easily readable.

◆ Check lighting in the room in advance of your presentation. Make sure that the room is light enough for participants to write while you're using the overhead, but also dark enough to see the transparencies easily.

◆ Use the biggest screen possible—a 10-by-10 foot screen is a minimum.

◆ Turn off the projector when there is a break between overheads of more than 15 seconds.

◆ Make sure your projected image fills the screen—use a fresh light bulb.

◆ Use catchy phrases on the screen during breaks—avoid wasting a chance to influence your audience. During "down time" you might put up a nature scene to relax the audience. Instead of missing the opportunity to make a statement during the breaks, put up a message like: "Change is easy," or "In a gentle way, you can shake the world."

◆ Avoid talking to the screen. Talk to the audience and look at the transparency itself if you need to see it.

◆ Use special laser pointer-markers. Avoid using your finger or hand to point.

◆ Have opening and closing overheads prepared. Be sure to use greetings on the overhead when people arrive and have a few closing ones, too. At the end, I use one like "Please complete feedback forms and leave them at the back table. Check for your personal items. Thank you. Have a safe drive home."

Hot Tips for Flip Charts and White Boards

1 Prepare flip charts and white boards ahead of time. If you want to write while the audience watches, pencil in points to remember.

2 Stand to the side while you write to insure that he audience has optimal viewing.

3 Prepare your presentation on flip charts on every other page. That way, you have a sequence prompter *and* you have room for spontaneity with the blank pages in-between. Plus, this better covers the next flip chart page.

4 Use thick pens that show up a good distance away.

5 Usually only the top two-thirds of the flip chart is visible to the entire audience. To increase the height of your stand, add leg extensions. Plastic PVC piping can be cut longer than the legs of the stand and then fitted over the legs to serve this purpose.

6 Only use flip charts and white board with groups that can easily see and read them. Generally, this means groups under 40 to 90 people. But it depends very strongly on chair set-up, elevation of the materials, content, and audience needs.

7 Limit what you write on flip charts and white boards to key words only.

8 If you can draw fairly well, draw icons or eye-catching illustrations to help boost audience attention and memory.

9 If you find yourself making out the same flip charts or white boards each presentation, turn the information into posters or overheads (anything more permanent); and save the hassle of doing it over each time. The more permanent visuals can be a worthwhile investment, especially if done in a very professional manner.

10 Post a flip chart on the side or back of the room and label it "Parking Lot." This flip chart should be divided into four quadrants labeled: 1) questions; 2) kudos; 3) Concerns/requests; and 4) networking. This provides the participants a board that they can add to. Have a supply of post-it notes near by that audience members can communicate with you on and post in the appropriate quadrant. Check the "Parking Lot" each day for notes and respond to each one. After you respond to the note, peel it off the board to leave room for others. You may want to save the notes to give you information for future presentations.

How can you improve your flip chart usage for your next presentation?

77 Ideas:

Insurance Policies

Things You Must Learn About Your Audience

1. Discover the make up of your audience in advance. What is their age, experience and specific job titles?

2. Is your audience's attendance voluntary or required?

3. What has happened in the past year, week, or 24 hours that might change their mindset about being at your training?

4. If you're traveling in from out of town, read the local newspaper to determine what the talk of the town is.

5. Arrive at your presentation early and talk to those who are there already. What are their concerns, issues, challenges?

6. Find out how far your attendees have come, how they like their jobs, and what they are happy or unhappy about. Learn their names.

7. When talking to audience members prior to the start of your presentation, seek information that you can use as personal examples in your talk.

Rapport is thought of as a mysterious "chemistry" that tells you if your audience is "with you." More technically, it is a distinct physiological state of positive responsiveness. With rapport you can lead you learners anywhere. Without it, you're likely to be ineffective and frustrated.

Ways to Prepare Your Audience

- Send your audience, in advance, a festive invitation as if they're being invited to a party. Include information like: directions, a theme, goals and what to wear.
- Send them a brief article that provides background or other pertinent information for the training.
- Create a short video that piques interest or gives an overview of your presentation.
- Send a brain teaser to each member of your audience to stimulate interest. It could be a jigsaw puzzle that needs the rest of the pieces to make sense or even a part of a story or article torn out of a larger article. This provides the frame work for a first day icebreaker—have members look for others who have the rest of their puzzle. This can also be one basis for forming teams.
- Send a pre-course survey to find out what the professional backgrounds are of your participants.
- Prepare a Top 10 List of FAQS (frequently asked questions) for your participants. Include the answers to questions like, "Do we get a workbook? Where are the bathrooms? When is lunch? Will it be fun? Will I be embarrassed? What if I have to miss a half day?
- Create a "Course survival guide" or "Participant's Fun Kit" for the program. You can include silly items like a stress reducing toy, a multi-colored pen, Post-its, a pair of Groucho glasses", a party horn, or an energy bar.
- Send audience members an audio tape with a greeting on it and even a theme song for the program. It can be as simple as a "theme song" from a pop group you like. For example, send a recording of "I Can't Get No Satisfaction" or "Simply the Best" for a customer service training.
- Send participants a book—one that absolutely fits the course you're offering. For example, when I do trainer's courses, I send this book. If it's a course on brain-compatible learning, I send a book called *Brain Facts*.
- Send participants course logistics, rules and an agenda in advance so that precious training time is saved from the outset. Avoid spending a lot of time on the dull stuff and take more time for the substantive training.
- Ask participants fill out a list of goals in advance. Learn about their needs and desires ahead of time so that you can better customize the training.

10 Problems Waiting to Happen

If it works for you financially, work with a partner or assistant. You'll appreciate having someone who can "put out fires" for you. This allows you to focus on the audience and the content and still have things run relatively smoothly.

If you are unable to bring an assistant, identify someone (usually it's your sponsor) who might act in this role. This person can be really helpful—especially in the following cases:

1 **To monitor a slamming door** (tape the noisy ones quiet!)

2 **To monitor the room temperature** (if it's wrong, everything's wrong!)

3 **To deal with competing distractions or noise.**

4 **To copy and coordinate additional handouts.**

5 **To attend to late arrivals** (personal emergencies, weather or traffic).

6 **To monitor lights** (for projection systems, visualization exercises, etc.).

7 **To assist with equipment malfunctions** (i.e., bulb out in your projection system, etc.).

8 **To arrange extra chairs or tables for late arrivals.**

9 **To insure name tags are received and worn.**

10 **To gather and bring people back from breaks on time.**

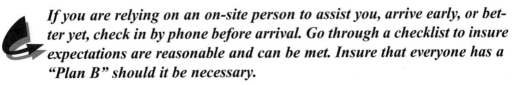

If you are relying on an on-site person to assist you, arrive early, or better yet, check in by phone before arrival. Go through a checklist to insure expectations are reasonable and can be met. Insure that everyone has a "Plan B" should it be necessary.

Item "To Do" List for Sponsors

A "To Do" list similar to the following example ought to be given to the host sponsor or organizer of your session.

◆ Have all participants been contacted and their registration confirmed. Has starting time and location been confirmed?

◆ Who will have access to the room and at what time can the presenter begin set up? Has somebody been identified to assist with the set up? Their name and phone number is:_____.

◆ In an emergency, who else can be notified? How?

◆ Who will be copying the course workbooks? Please see that only on one side of the paper is copied so that participants can use the other side for notes. Please copy 10 to 20 percent more than number of registrants.

◆ My introduction will be sent to you under separate cover on:_____.

◆ Please provide for the following music/sound system requirements:_____.

◆ Please have the sound system pre-tested and set for operation by:_____.

◆ Please provide a sturdy flip chart stand with a full pad of paper.

◆ Please provide a full set of fresh colored markers containing three in dark colors (black, blue, brown).

◆ Please provide an overhead projector that has been pre-tested and set for operation by: (please insure the illumination is bright and that it is positioned to fill the screen).

◆ Please provide a spare bulb for the overhead projector should it be needed. Is the projector lens and glass clean?

◆ Please provide a screen that is at least 10 feet by 10 feet.

◆ Please provide one pre-tested stationary microphone (have this set up for use if the group size exceeds 60 people). Hand-held mikes are not recommended unless it's a very formal presentation.

◆ Please provide for the following additional audio-visual. equipment: (film projector, slide projector, computer stand, VCR and monitor, TV, extension cord, etc.)

◆ Please monitor the room temperature so that it remains between 65 and 70 degrees, unless otherwise notified.

◆ Should the temperature need adjusting, who is responsible?

◆ Please arrange for coffee, tea, ice water and juice service in the morning and soft drinks, water or juice for the mid-afternoon break.

◆ Please prepare the room and audience seating as indicated in the enclosed diagram. Arrange set up to be completed by:_____.

◆ Thank you for your support. If you have any questions, please contact me at: _____(office number and/or home).

Are there things you would like to add to the "to do" list?

Ways to Manage the Micro-Details

It may seem that there are a million details to plan for when organizing a training; there are! But if you have a "B" plan in place for nearly everything, you can offset many troubles. Consider the following pointers when managing the micro-details of an out-of-town presentation:

◆ How will your handouts get to the training? Will they be copied once you arrive at your destination or can you send the master copy in advance with instructions for your host to prepare them? What are your alternatives?

◆ Do you have a back-up alarm clock system? What if you have a power outage and your wake-up alarm is disarmed?

◆ How will you be getting to the airport? Have you made the necessary arrangements?

◆ What if your transportation breaks down? Do you have a cell-phone and contact numbers should you need to seek help?

◆ What if your flight is delayed? Do you know the alternative flights? Will you be able to contact the person who will be meeting you at the airport?

◆ Are you booked on the last flight of the day to your particular destination? If so, would an overnight delay disrupt your plans?

◆ Have you considered the weather? Would bad weather disrupt any segment of the training? Are you planning on being outside for any part of it?

◆ If your luggage were to be lost, could you still do your presentation? Do you have a secondary plan in mind should this happen?

◆ Do you have the essentials for your presentation in a carry-on bag? Could the rest be purchased in time if necessary?

◆ Have you arranged transportation once you arrive at your destination? If you've reserved a rental car, what will you do if the agency has overbooked?

◆ Is it possible for you to arrive one day in advance if traveling from out of town?

◆ Have you arranged to check out the room where you'll be speaking ahead of time? Who will be your contact? What authority do they have?

◆ Do you have whatever you normally use to relax with you?

- Have you made it a point to build relationships with your host and the staff who will be assisting?

- Have you asked yourself, "What would make this room optimal?"

- If the room is different than your original request, what will you do?

- Do you have a secondary plan in place should you be sick and not able to make the presentation? What if you have a sore throat?

- What is the room like where the presentation will be held? How many will be in attendance?

- Do you have a list of the people in charge, their contact numbers and roles? Where will you meet them?

- What about lunch? What about breaks?

- Where are the bathrooms? How many are there compared to the group size? Are there alternative bathrooms?

- What if the electronic equipment (computer, overhead, video or music player) breaks down? Do you have an alternative?

- What is the parking situation like? Will you or your participants have trouble parking? Is there a charge for parking?

- Where is the drinking fountain? Will there be water available throughout your presentation?

- Have you talked to the person who is responsible for the Audio/Visual equipment? What is there experience?

- Where are telephones located? Are there enough so that a line doesn't form at the break?

- Who will be controlling the lighting? Will the audio-visual tech be responsible for the lighting, as well?

- Where are electrical outlets located? Are there enough? If not, can you arrange for a surge-control multiple outlet unit?

- Where can you find logistical support? Who is in charge of registration?

- Have you covered all the bases? Taken nothing for granted and personally checked out everything yourself?

Starting Off on the Right Foot

6 Openers to Avoid

Do whatever is necessary to avoid these presentation killers:

1 Starting Late

Even if you don't start on time, when it is the time to start, tell the audience when you will start. For example, you might say, "Thank you for being here on time. There's been an emergency at the Interstate near our hotel. Only half our group's here. We'll be starting just 10 minutes from now. Until that time, please review your course materials and you can look forward to a great day."

2 Unexpected Introductory Remarks

If your sponsor will be introducing you, prepare the introduction for them. If this is not possible, ask if you may review their introduction. Introductory remarks that are not aligned with your message or that damage your credibility will not get your presentation off to a good start.

3 An Equipment Failure

Have room set-up completed at least a couple of hours in advance, or more, if possible. This will give you enough time to replace anything if necessary and to double check the operation of all equipment.

4 Starting Without the Audience's Attention

If your audience is not ready to start and it's time, have a plan to get their attention. Something novel or multi-sensory will stimulate their interest. Do not just demand their attention by saying something like: "May I have your attention up here?" Get creative.

5 Starting With an Apology

This is a weak way to start. If you feel the need to apologize for something, avoid making it your first words. Instead, start with offering value. If you're late or your equipment took extra time and it is your fault, greet the audience first, commend them for something (their enthusiasm, promptness, colorful appearance, etc.), apologize quickly and then jump right into an active and energetic start.

6 Starting Too Slowly

Always start with enthusiasm and energy! The more senses you can engage right from the start, the more your audience will follow your lead. Our brain loves to be stimulated!

7 Great Ways to Get Started

1 Provide an Overview

Give your audience a road map of your presentation from the start. If they know what to expect, they relax without wondering: 1) if you know where you're going; 2) if you're credible; 3) if they should trust you; and/or 4) if they'll learn anything.

2 Involve Your Audience

Elicit from learners what possible value and relevance your presentation has to them. Learners have to feel connected to the topic to benefit from it. Giving audience members the opportunity to express themselves can make a huge difference in their willingness to get involved. This can be done in small groups or in the large group.

3 Provide Multi-Sensory Stimulation

Show a short video that captures the essence of your message; use puppets, music, flip charts or other dramatic aids, such as slides, videos, special effect sounds, multi-media, plus anything else your creativity provides.

4 Offer Something Concrete

The brain learns particularly well from concrete experiences first. Provide something real, physical or concrete. This can be in the form of a prop, a real-life dilemma, an experiment, etc.

5 Do Something Novel

The optimum "hook" is a novel or surprising experience that meets strong personal learner needs and taps into curiosity and real life themes.

6 Tell a True Story

Give a true life example or read an exceptional parable or story that creates a strong immediate connection.

7 Make Expectations Explicit

Tell the audience what they can expect from your presentation. Share with them your own expectations for the day. Be specific. For example, tell them, "By the end of today, you can expect to have 20 concrete strategies to improve your memory."

5 Things to Say in the First 30 Seconds

While audience is getting seated, play some inspiring music. When you are ready to begin the presentation, proceed with your attention-getting strategy. Once you have captured the audience's interest, proceed with your introduction.

1 Greet the Audience

Tell them you're excited to join them. "Good morning...I'm Eric Jensen. It's a pleasure to be here today."

2 Present the Topic

Give the name or title of the talk or course you're facilitating. "The title of our brief session today is, 'Training with the Brain in Mind'."

3 Present a "Hook"

"Today you'll discover the three most important things you can do that boost intrinsic motivation, understanding and greater job success. If that's of interest to you, raise your hand and say 'Yes'!"

4 Facilitate an Icebreaker

"Before we get started, let's wake up the body with a quick stretch. Please stand up..." Or, "Before we jump in, let's find out who our neighbors are. Please introduce yourself to three other people and tell them what you do." Or, "To get ourselves going, everyone will need a ballot to do some voting on. Rather than having everyone come up front to get a ballot, choose one person in each group of four or five to be the runner. Why don't you do that now."

5 Other Options

The first 30 seconds of your presentation will characterize the entire day. Some other options include: telling a brief story of something true that happened to you lately; giving an amazing bit of factual trivia: "Did you know that...?"; sharing a particularly appropriate quotation; opening with a quiz or survey; asking an outrageous question of the audience; or telling a humorous joke (if it's tried and true and good!) Remember to over-rehearse your first 30 seconds.

Rules for Positive Openings

1 Make your greeting warm, friendly and inviting. Let them know you care. Be generous with your eye contact.

2 Do something fun immediately. Conduct a brief stretching exercise, a freebie giveaway, or a bingo game.

3 Make sure that your posture and positioning says that you like speaking to groups, and you're open to your participants.

4 Get others involved. Simply say, "Now that I've introduced myself, would you please introduce yourself to others? Turn to the person next to you and say, 'Good morning, glad you're here.'" Or, "I'll give you a moment; please greet the person on each side of you." Typically, people will be cooperative and friendly in response to your request.

5 Use humor. Be careful though. Know the rules: it must be simple, short, understandable by everyone, and offensive to none.

6 Ask a question that elicits a positive state in the group. Sometimes I will simply ask a leading question like: "How many of you would not only like to have a valuable session today, but also would like to really have fun?"

How do you plan on opening your next presentation?

Instant Icebreakers

1 Stretch

Start with some simple stretching. You can do this in the large group or break into smaller groups and have each choose a leader to guide them for three to five minutes. Use music.

2 Baby Pictures

Ask each audience member to send in a baby picture in advance. Number the back of them to identify whose they are. Display the pictures at the training and ask participants to guess who is who.

3 Name Tag Switch

Have everyone write three to five descriptive qualifiers on their name tag like: "energetic, piano-playing, computer savvy, runner." Collect them all and pass them out randomly. Give the group time to locate the owner of the mystery name tag.

4 Hats

Make a silly, funky hat (like a newspaper hat) on the first day and introduce yourself (wearing it) with a smile. Give a quick biography of yourself.

5 Wanted Posters

Each audience member makes a wanted poster without their name on it that describes themselves: hobbies, height, hair color, last seen, etc. After everyone posts their sign, audience members can guess who the wanted person is throughout the workshop. They can write their guess at the bottom of the poster.

6 Shoe Sort

Everyone forms a circle with their chairs and puts their shoes in the center of the circle. Each person gets a turn to pick up a shoe and try to guess the owner of it and why they guessed that person. This is best done with a group that knows each other at least some.

7 Fact or Fib

Everyone gets an index card. They put their name on it with three facts and three lies about themselves. After pairing up and switching cards with their partner, each tries to figure out which items are the truth and which are fibs.

8 Puppets

Audience members each receive a hand puppet (or a cheap sock or paper bag if you're on a budget). The game is to assign a character to the puppet that represents someone at work; and then have the puppet introduce them to the rest of the group. This can be done in small groups if the audience is large.

9 Stand and Go

You say, "All those who like classical music (or Chinese food or jazz, or pizza, or chocolate or travel or German cars, etc.) please go to this corner. Then say, "All those who like rock n' roll (or Italian food or chicken or waffles or Italian cars, etc.) go to a different corner." Once you have the audience in about five groups, let them meet each other and share what they have in common. Then, if time permits, you can remix pairs again.

Describe an icebreaker here that you have adapted for the classroom?

8 Ways to Warm a Resistant Audience

1 Make the room inviting with music, flowers and posters.

2 Ask questions that are open ended and opinion oriented in order to reduce the fear of being wrong. Be accepting and positive about your audience's remarks.

3 Be affirming in your responses. Let people know that you value their opinions. Demonstrate a caring attitude. Enjoy your audience.

4 Insure that participants know your expectations. Tell the audience when you prefer to field questions and how to get your attention. Take their fear or stress out of the event.

5 Assure the audience that you want their involvement. Give them specific vehicles for input. These might include: access to you at the breaks, a place to put written questions for you, or a time designated to ask.

6 Make minor mistakes, and role-model your comfort with them. Make a joke directed at yourself, although, make sure that its not really belittling.

7 Whatever your greeting, put energy into it! It could be "Good morning," or "Hi, and welcome to...." Congruence is critical at this time. Make sure your verbal message is also conveyed by your body language and gestures.

8 Use words in their positive form! Avoid negatives (i.e., "We're not going to get stressed out today by the traffic"). Put goodies on their chair or table—affirmations, mini-chocolate bars, a kazoo, or special invitations.

Audience De-stressors

1 Lead some stretching set to music. Tell the audience about the value of stress reduction and stretching. Ask them to break into small groups and choose a leader if your audience is large.

2 Allow for small group discussions so participants can air anything that is on their minds. It might be sharing time, gripe time, or a current events topic.

3 Ask everyone to pair up with a partner and take a five-minute walk outside (if weather permits). Give them a topic to share about or have them make one up. I often ask them to share what they're grateful for, what they've learned lately, their promise for the day, or their most pressing concern.

4 Set aside group journal-writing time. This can be done formally or informally with either an assigned topic or a topic of the learner's choice.

5 Facilitate a large group discussion. Allow participants to raise any issue they want. Write the issues up on the board or flip chart. After everyone has expressed themselves, review the issues and address as many of them as possible. Some of them will relate to each other and can be handled at once. If necessary, problem-solving or resolution strategies to the issues can continue to be discussed in small groups who then report back to the large group.

What other kinds of de-stressor activities have you conducted in your presentations?

75 Ideas:
Building Good
Relationships

Audience Relationship-Builders

The audience doesn't care how much you know until they know how much you care.

◆ With a large group, use the technique of eye contact rotation when you begin speaking. This involves looking at just one person at a time for a few seconds. First pick someone on the left side deep, then the right side close up, then move to the left side close-up, then the right side deep, and start the rotation again throughout your talk.

◆ With a small group, also use eye contact; however, start by making contact with people you've met before or faces that look familiar. Once you feel less stressed and more confident, begin to make eye contact with the unfamiliar faces.

◆ Talk about what you have in common; the weather, parking problems, an election, other people, etc.

◆ Empathize with your audience; let them know that you care about their feelings, challenges and particular circumstances.

◆ Share something personal or close to your heart—a family situation, etc.

◆ Treat every audience member with respect, always.

◆ Tell a human interest story.

◆ Share examples of how you have handled a past situation.

◆ Answer the learner's question, "What's in it for me?"

◆ Let the learners tell you what they want to learn and hook into that.

◆ Give learners the opportunity to ask questions, share something relevant, or comment on the material you're covering.

◆ Share a story about how a past participant has used their learning from the training.

◆ Let the audience know that you've done (or do) the same kind of work they do (only if it's true).

◆ Start off with linking learning to a recent current event.

◆ Tap into the values common to the demographics of your learners.

25 Ways to Achieve Credibility

◆ Learn your material inside and out.

◆ Stay abreast of changes, discoveries, or innovations in your field.

◆ Share with others the number of years you've done what you do; expound briefly on your experience; or naturally integrate into your presentation experiences you've obtained in your field.

◆ Integrate information into your talk like companies you've worked for, national projects you've been involved in, and/or universities you've attended.

◆ Name your mentors or mention well-known people in your specialty area.

◆ Join professional organizations in your field.

◆ Nurture relationships with media people and public figures.

◆ Send out press releases to media contacts regarding an event you're coordinating or your involvement in one.

◆ Do a radio or TV interview.

◆ Volunteer for committees, studies or organization work related to your field.

◆ Write a book or make an audio tape. Publish it yourself if necessary.

◆ Attend key conferences. Speak at them if possible.

◆ Write an article to be published in a journal, newsletter, tape, or bulletin related to your area of specialty.

◆ Associate with people of high stature in your field.

◆ Know most of the significant theories in your specialty area.

- Be early, or on time. Personally check all electronic and technical equipment.

- Share your vision boldly with the audience; be "cutting edge" in your subject area niche.

- Use voice modulation or microphone if needed; give clear instructions.

- Be careful to back-up claims or statements. Cite references.

- Know your audience well; customize your presentation to each audience.

- Know the time limits and keep to them unless negotiated with the audience.

- Avoid unusual or different clothing that the audience might label odd.

- Never assume something about a person in your audience (i.e., if you ask a woman what she does and she tells you she's in the medical field, don't assume that she's a nurse. She very well may be a doctor.

- Light-hearted jokes that poke fun at yourself can be perceived as confidence.

- Avoid buzz words or hot buttons or undefined acronyms that others might not understand or approve of.

What kinds of things have you done to establish your professional credibility?

Habits That Spell Professionalism

- Always be passionate about your topic.

- Use positive language, never use vulgarity, profanity, racist or sexist remarks.

- Dress professionally, culturally appropriate, stylish, and dressier than your audience.

- Observe protocol: respect others; no put-downs. Don't dismiss questions or concerns flippantly. Say something good or not at all.

- Purses or briefcases, jewelry and accessories should be classy, modest and subtle.

- Use portable phones tactfully, out of social circles; use laptop computers in appropriate settings.

- If you don't know the answer to a question, say so. Don't speculate. Instead, explain that you'll find out the answer and get back to the person, or give a suggestion for where the answer can be found.

- Shake hands with people firmly.

- Keep to your agreements, tell the truth, be supportive, follow the rules.

- Listen to others carefully, be an active listener, and remember the names of key people.

- Honor the culture of your audience with your gestures, habits, references, words, introductions, materials and closings.

- Know who the experts in your field are and associate yourself with them.

- Use up-to-date content and have structure of presentation thoroughly organized.

◆ Use success stories of others or tell of a personal failure that resulted in you becoming a better person.

◆ Use classy materials, overheads, and props.

◆ Handle hecklers and distractions with tact and ease.

◆ Avoid copying other people's materials; develop your own show.

◆ Read a new book in your field every month.

◆ Be politically correct. Don't make gross generalizations about groups of people or use off-color jokes at other's expense.

◆ Include a bibliography in your handouts.

◆ Don't discount complaints or concerns from the audience. Provide excellent "customer" service.

◆ Be fully present and positive with the audience; leave personal problems at home.

◆ Acknowledge the people who were instrumental in making your presentation happen.

◆ Never act like a stuck-up star, even if you are considered the "expert."

Can you think of any other ways to achieve or maintain your professionalism?

Personal Rapport-Builders

1 Polite observations: "Beautiful jacket."

2 Shared opinions and beliefs: "Laughing is great medicine; and you don't have to see the doctor to get a prescription for it!"

3 Information shared: "Did you know that Rodney Dangerfield was a stand-up comedian for 20 years before he was 'discovered'?"

4 Feelings shared: "I feel very nervous speaking to a group of comedians..."

5 Dreams, goals, needs, wishes shared: "Someday I'd like to write the great American novel."

6 Activities shared: "I've got three dogs at home that keep me running whether I want to or not. In fact, we ran our first half-marathon together last weekend."

7 Relate something from your past that relates to this particular audience: "My first gig as a stand-up comedian was at a senior-citizens home in 1979... Most of the audience had lost their hearing, so I was a hit!"

8 Relate something from your present that relates to this particular group: "I'm writing a piece for Reader's Digest right now that advocates comedy tapes as part of the treatment package for stroke survivors."

9 Relationships shared: You know, my mother-in-law Josie Albright, was instrumental in my evolution from comedian to trainer. When she moved in with us, a day job became very attractive. No really, as a corporate trainer for IBM for many years, her experience has proven invaluable to me. Last month, in fact, she introduced me to Stephen Covey, author of *The Seven Habits of Highly Effective People.*"

10 Ask about them; then listen without interrupting. "What inspired you to come to this training?"

160 Ideas: Insuring Optimal Learning

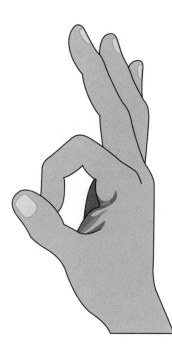

11 Ways to Enhance the Learning Process

1 Create discussion groups with specific agendas or subjects to discuss.

2 Have learners create a research project on a topic related to the current theme.

3 Ask learners to tie learning together thematically.

4 Have learners write, ask or design review questions.

5 Ask learners to team up; and re-group with a different partner.

6 Have learners read up on the topic or watch a video.

7 Learners can sort, analyze or make mind maps of the material.

8 Ask audience to create a game like bingo or jeopardy.

9 Create a forum, debate, skit, or musical rendition of the learning.

10 Rely on the collective knowledge and wisdom of your audience.

11 Role-reversal—participants play the presenter's role.

Ideas for Productive Processing Time

Processing time or "down time" is essential for the learner to make meaning out of what has been learned.

◆ **Journal writing**

◆ **15-minute coffee or water break**

◆ **Note-taking time**

◆ **Small group work with loose agenda**

◆ **Lunch break**

◆ **Watch a review video**

◆ **Personal relaxation**

◆ **Listen to calming music**

◆ **Afternoon break**

◆ **Stand and stretch for a minute**

◆ **Choice time to work on any project**

◆ **Reflection time**

◆ **On a multi-day course, go home and reflect**

◆ **Possibly a change of subjects**

Ways to Deepen Learning

◆ Acquisition learning: participants simply "pick up" learning unconsciously from the environment—posters, observations, nonverbals, demonstrations or exhibitions.

◆ Affirmations: these can be visual, auditory or kinesthetic.

◆ Brainstorming: generating or gathering a large quantity of ideas.

◆ Case histories: study a real life situation and learn from it or solve it.

◆ Challenge course: outdoor ropes course is one example. Some companies have developed portable challenge courses that can be brought to your site.

◆ Choice: give your audience a choice of activities or in the selection of them.

◆ Computers: some software programs provide highly interactive, visual, and auditory learning methods.

◆ Cooperative groups: problem-solving exercises and group projects.

◆ Discussions: encourage everyone's contributions; the value is in the process, as well as the content.

◆ Debates: have learners choose relevant topics.

◆ Demonstrations: participants present to the large group.

◆ Discovery: an opportunity to experience boundary-less learning.

◆ Drilling: useful only if it's novel, fun, and non-threatening.

◆ Exams: have learners design them. The value is in designing them, not taking them.

◆ Exhibitions: displays and products provide a kinesthetic and interesting way to learn about content.

◆ Experience: always follow-up and experiential learning exercise with a debriefing or group sharing.

◆ Feedback: ought to be frequent, specific, and timely.

◆ Field trips: increase novelty, relevance, and real-life learning. Can be as simple as going to a job site or even using a different room than usual.

◆ Guest speakers: bring in speakers from the community.

◆ Games: build trust, teamwork, risk-taking, creativity, support and leadership.

◆ Hands-on learning: on the job, in-context learning where the angles converge to create more meaning.

◆ Imagery: visualization supplements the process of learning dramatically.

◆ Interviews: participants can interview each other or experts or guest speakers.

◆ News: copy and discuss an article on a relevant topic.

◆ Multi-age/cross-job tutoring: peer training.

- Inventories: personality profiles or learning style profiles where learners self-assess their knowledge, skills, strengths and weaknesses.
- Jigsaws: learning process which starts in a group, then individuals spread out to learn independently, then return to share with the group.
- Joint meetings: meet with participants individually to build on content and process of learning.
- Learning stations: provides choice and independent learning. Organize by topic or theme and learning style.
- Lecturettes: mini-lectures of 10-minutes or less. Include processing time, too.
- Mind-Mapping: a form of visual thinking which provides many tools for learning.
- Mentors: can provide superior role models for learning through example.
- Metaphors: can appeal to the subconscious or nonconscious mind.
- Models: allow participants to build a real working model of the process.
- Organizing information: rank or prioritize related information.
- Overhead transparencies: presents a visual for greetings, directions, affirmations, pictures.
- Panel discussions: can generate critical questions and explore them in-depth from various viewpoints.
- Participant presentations: can be given to the whole group or just a few.
- Peer presenting: in dyads or small groups.
- Peer support: rituals that build a sense of a learning community.
- Projects: are a complex and satisfying way to learn.
- Questions: ask participants to generate a list of relevant questions.
- Quiet time: for reflection to sort out experiences and debrief learning.
- Reading: providing choice of reading material is good and processing time is critical.
- Repetition: check first, provide feedback, then proceed.
- Reports: these can be created and given a dozen ways. Keep the stakes high.
- Research: gives the learner challenge, freedom, satisfaction and accountability.
- Risk-taking: might be something artistic, physical or a new intellectual concept.
- Self-directed: learners choose their project, goals, methods and output.
- Simulations: design learning activities that feel like the real thing.
- Teamwork: create some low-stress competition or play a game.
- Videos: can illuminate the points you're making, or use one to record events.
- Walks: pair up and go for a reflective, sharing 10 minute walk outside.
- Written self-plans: develop a month-long personal plan for mastery of content.

Active Processing Strategies

◆ Compare and contrast new learning with prior learning.

◆ Mind-map the material; then re-do the original mind-map from memory.

◆ Visualize the material and make picture links.

◆ Draw a visual of what's been learned—use a Venn diagram, fishbone or flow chart.

◆ Analyze a problem or do a case study.

◆ Match up the learning with a set of criteria—possibly a check list or rubric.

◆ Generate ideas about the topic—possible new applications of the material.

◆ Read a chunk of material and locate key ideas in it.

◆ Create test questions for the speaker.

◆ Write in a journal or learning log. A good process for identifying agreements and disagreements with the material, to personalize the learning or draw conclusions about it.

◆ Distribute a survey on a topic and let learners compile the results.

◆ Set up a team review. Divide the whole group in half and give one-half an article or handout to read in a separate location. When they return after the time limit, have them discuss the article with a partner from the other half of the group. The tasks can be reversed the second time through.

◆ Do a whole group choral review. Give learners a prompt; they finish the response.

◆ Give learners index cards with various topics written on them or questions for them to think about or ask out loud to the group.

Thinking Activities

◆ Make links to other related ideas and topics using visual tools.

◆ Predict possible short- and long-term consequences.

◆ Re-state the material in own words. Create a position paper.

◆ Combine material; make guesses how it would be understood by another person in another location or circumstance.

◆ Provide counter arguments to the material; debate it.

◆ Generate examples of the learning and sort them.

◆ Apply use of information learned to the real-world.

◆ Discuss an article on the topic with **no boundaries** (open session).

◆ Compare your own interpretations and notes with another persons.

◆ Interview a partner; they can assume a role and become an expert on the topic or just share what they learned.

◆ Edit or critique someone else's work.

◆ Create questions for the facilitator or for a test.

◆ Review the topic or preview the next one.

◆ Build an abstract or working model of the topic or solution.

◆ Piece together or solve some kind of jigsaw puzzle.

Mind-Mapping Techniques

If you learn best visually, you may want to use mind-mapping. Mind-mapping is a technique where the learner organizes the subject in a pattern of connected ideas. Similar to a sentence diagram, a road map or a blueprint, the learner uses their creativity and understanding of the topic to draw a map of it.

◆ **The topic is highlighted on a large piece of paper.**

◆ **Branches for key sub-topics can be added.**

◆ **Add details to the branches.**

◆ **Personalize it for the "right brain."**

◆ **Branches might be labeled with chapter headings, or sub-topics.**

◆ **Bold-face print, upper and lower case, or all caps can be used to distinguish among categories.**

◆ **Pictures and symbols can be used for key ideas.**

◆ **Use creativity. Let your brain out to play.**

◆ **Multiple colors and/or arrows can be used to show relationships.**

◆ **Various mediums can be used to add interest or detail.**

◆ **Use personal examples; make it relevant.**

◆ **Add to your mind map a day later.**

◆ **Keep testing your recall to uncover weaknesses and build on strengths.**

Ways to Provide More Feedback

◆ Utilize pre-established criteria from which learners can self-assess.

◆ Hold discussion groups to evaluate learning.

◆ Pair up and present to another what's been learned.

◆ Use partners and teammates to critique another's work.

◆ Provide a list of clear criteria for success and use a checklist.

◆ Use audiotape or videotape and let groups review their performances.

◆ Offer time for self-correction, reflection, or journal writing.

◆ Devise simple outlines for self-assessment, scoring and analysis.

◆ Learners compare their intended goals and objectives with end results.

◆ Hold a discussion where learners get ideas validated or shaped.

◆ Conduct debates or mock quiz shows.

◆ Learners generate solo or shared mind-maps.

◆ Facilitator observations.

◆ Assign projects where the results of the effort provide feedback.

◆ Create work that others in the community can benefit from or add to.

◆ Learners talk themselves through their thinking, out loud.

◆ Participants keep score charts for their team and post the results.

◆ Have learners work together to create a performance review or test.

◆ Have learners self-correct their work.

◆ Learners present to the group and get oral or written feedback.

12 Strategies to Enhance Verification

◆ Participants create a presentation with presenting tools.

◆ Mind-map the material; pass it around for peer review.

◆ Provide question and answer time, a panel discussion, or a group dialogue.

◆ The participant designs questions for a test, then the presenter interviews the participant.

◆ Use both a written assessment and a verbal assessment.

◆ The participant creates a project—a working model, a mind map, a video, a newsletter, etc.

◆ Create a video and use it as a teaching tool.

◆ The participant presents a lecturette lesson to the class.

◆ Role-play, simulations, or skits are especially good for integrating learning.

◆ Hold group discussions.

◆ Practice "simulated "expert" interviews.

◆ Play games which require content knowledge like a quiz show.

 Most of what is important to the brain, that which truly shapes our understanding, out thinking, our meaning and our character, is relatively difficult to access.

7 ways to Celebrate the Learning

1 Celebration needs to engage learner emotions - have a toast with sparking apple cider (or Champagne if appropriate). Make it fun, light and joyful.

2 It's bragging time or peer sharing. Learners demonstrate their work and give acknowledgments to each other.

3 Dancing—do square, line or party dancing. Include everyone. The focus ought to be on enjoyment, not technique.

4 Music, streamers, and compliments can be part of the celebration.

5 It can be as simple as giving another a "high-five."

6 Create party hats and do a potluck with dessert foods.

7 Have the group plan, design, and produce a celebration party.

Acknowledgement is a key component of celebrating learning; how do you acknowledge your learners?

72 Ideas:

Facilitating
Great
Audience
Interactions:

Most Common Threats to Avoid

When participants feel threatened, in any way, their interactions are impaired and diminished. Here are some of the most common threats.

1 Opinions of Others

Audience members worry what others will think of their comments, questions, and/or contributions, and what the presenter thinks of them.

2 An Upcoming Evaluation or Test

Learners will worry the most if they think you might "pop" an unexpected quiz on them. A second big worry is an unfair quiz or test.

3 Having to Perform Publicly

Very few people like to public speak. Any assignments, therefore, which require learners to make a presentation need to be fair, fun, and not a surprise.

4 Lack of Resources

Participants might lack materials, time, support or technology to do the assigned task.

5 Impossible Deadlines

In order to do their best work, people need time to prepare.

6 Public Criticism

No one likes being criticized; insure that this never happens in your sessions.

7 Awkward Groupings

This includes being on teams or in pairs that are uncomfortable.

8 Potential Failure

Failure in private is bad enough; failure exposed to a whole group is even worse.

9 Potential Embarrassment

Embarrassment can happen in nearly any circumstance. Reduce the possibility of it as much as possible in your sessions.

Tips for Creating a Safe Climate

The following tips might sound like simple common sense suggestions. But sometimes, common sense is not so common.

◆ **Never ask a participant to speak unless he or she volunteers, or they have had time to prepare.**

◆ **Never mock or embarrass a participant, even if they make a silly or stupid mistake.**

◆ **Never mock a culture, class, race, religion, gender, or lifestyle.**

◆ **Make sure everyone has access to understandable instructions and expectations.**

◆ **Avoid using nicknames, judgment names, or stereotype labels, even in jest.** (i.e., slow learners or turtles, lazy brains, show-off, etc.).

◆ **Use the words, "please" and "thank you" as well as "I'm sorry."**

◆ **Make sure all learners have the resources to learn including something to write with and on.**

◆ **Insure that everyone understood your directions and assignments by repeating them and posting them visually.**

◆ **Avoid making any negative comments about another person** (i.e., their looks, clothing, accent, abilities, personality, etc.).

◆ **Don't ask people to share a joke publicly unless they volunteer.**

◆ **Always give people the option of "passing" on a particular assignment, task, exercise, or request. Give them an acceptable alternative.**

Deadly Audience Mistakes to Avoid

1 Assuming you know about the audience when you don't.

2 Being arrogant or acting like too much of an expert.

3 Not knowing the local, company, neighborhood, or town culture.

4 Not learning about your audience and what they already know.

5 Using buzz words that may be outdated or banned.

6 Telling off-color, racist, sexist, or derogatory jokes.

7 Wearing inappropriate clothing.

8 Referring negatively to stars, heroes, bosses, or local icons.

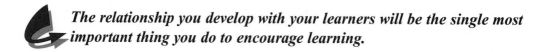

The relationship you develop with your learners will be the single most important thing you do to encourage learning.

4 Ways to Answer Tough Questions and Preserve Credibility

1 Let the audience know in advance if and when you'll be fielding questions.

2 Repeat all questions. If not word-for-word, insure that your restated question is accurate.

3 Make eye contact with the person asking the question when you begin the answer and end it. Look at other audience members in between.

4 If you don't know the answer to the question, say so. But don't make a big deal out of it. Simply respond with any of the following or a similar response:

- ◆ "Sorry, I'm not knowledgeable about that area; I'll have to look that one up."
- ◆ "I'll have to check my references on that question, and get back to you. Is that OK with you?"
- ◆ "Boy, that's one I wish I knew. Thanks for asking."
- ◆ "Sorry, that question is outside my expertise; but I'll bet you could find some interesting information on it at the university library."

 Always handle an irritated participant. Listen, empathize, and respect the learner's point of view.

Non-Verbal Rapport-Building Strategies

1 Smile and show your audience you like them even before you start.

2 Establish individual rapport with key persons or group leaders as soon as possible.

3 Observe the breathing rate of key people by watching for the rise and fall of the shoulders. Match that rate with your own breathing.

4 Notice gestures of others you're communicating with, such as: a tapping foot, a flicking pencil, a rocking posture or similar methodical movements. Then begin your own gestures of a different type, using the identical tempo.

5 Notice postures of others such as slumped shoulders, tilt head, rigidly upright, or crossed legs or arms. Match the posture.

6 Match or mirror facial expressions along with eye movements and patterns.

7 Align your physical energy with the group—be willing to follow, as well as lead.

The most important clues you'll get from your students are non-verbal: posture, breathing, tonality, tempo, gestures, etc. These behaviors are critical to monitor because most persons are unaware of them - meaning they are accurate indicators of where you stand with another.

Verbal Tools for Quick Rapport-Building

◆ Start with what you have in common with your audience and build on that.

◆ Get-to-know each other through the sharing of personal experiences.

◆ Find matches through common values like security, ambition, goals, etc.

◆ Change conversational "buts" to "ands."

◆ Don't disagree, rather extend ideas.

◆ Match verbals: voice tempo, tonality and volume.

◆ Match superlatives: "hot" or "cool" or "fantastic."

◆ Change from using "I" and "you" words to "we" and "us" words.

◆ Match approximate physical height by sitting, standing, or bending.

◆ Acknowledge the other person's ideas so they know they are valued.

◆ Ask for the other person's opinion and give them credit for it.

◆ Get to "yes sets" by starting with agreement on easy topics—seek common ground.

◆ Show interest in and be curious about the other person's world by asking gentle questions. Don't probe or put people on the spot.

◆ Match v-a-k (visual, auditory or kinesthetic) modalities with predicates like: "I see what you mean, that sounds good, or that feels right."

First Aid Tips for Heckled Presenters

First, Discover If:

◆ The heckler is primarily expressing an emotion. If "yes," then make sure you listen to hear it out. If "no," answer the comment simply.

◆ The heckler is alone or do many others concur? If alone, deal with it quickly or at a break. If others concur, deal with it as a group, as soon as possible.

Then, Take Action:

◆ Take in a slow deep breath.

◆ Think of "being of service."

◆ Provide short specific answers.

◆ Avoid asking, "What's wrong?"

◆ Ask, "What would make it right?"

◆ Keep your interactions brief.

◆ Avoid a battle or a "crazy-making" confrontation.

◆ Make your response a public promise if need be.

◆ If you need more time, set a time for later.

◆ Always make a final check to insure asker is satisfied.

◆ Re-elicit positive learning state with rest of group before starting up again.

6 Questioning Strategies

1 Provide a "mistakes okay" safe climate; admit your own first.

2 Assert that there are likely multiple answers to the questions you ask.

3 Phrase questions for open-ended and multiple responses: i.e., "Customer service is always important. What are some of the ways companies are improving it?"

4 Check in with your audience before asking questions to insure readiness.

5 Ask learners to work or review in teams or with partners; this keeps the pressure off individuals.

6 Utilize three boxes of understanding: ask learners if they believe they have: 1) vague; 2) average; or 3) expert understanding of the topic.

> *The better the quality of the questions asked, the more the brain is challenged to think. What are some engaging questions you ask your learners?*

Engaging the Learner

26 Ways to Motivate Learners

- ◆ Remove threats; make the environment emotionally safe.
- ◆ Tease with curiosity about the content.
- ◆ Use a variety of learning styles.
- ◆ Set goals together—develop ownership.
- ◆ Create powerful recall.
- ◆ Engage emotions.
- ◆ Tell learners how they will succeed—provide the rules.
- ◆ Take frequent stretch breaks.
- ◆ Use multiple intelligences.
- ◆ Celebrate successes.
- ◆ Treat everybody with respect.
- ◆ Go multi-media and multi-sensory.
- ◆ Credit learners with good ideas.
- ◆ Respect cultural differences.
- ◆ Keep learning relevant; give specific real-life examples.
- ◆ Counter negative barriers with positive responses.
- ◆ Provide choice and variety.
- ◆ Use the power of suggestion for transitions, state changes, and challenges.
- ◆ Provide learning tools like computers; and individual assistance if needed.
- ◆ Invite breakthroughs.
- ◆ Role-model a love of learning.
- ◆ Draw out past successes.
- ◆ Increase learner feedback.
- ◆ Involve learners constantly.
- ◆ Insure that the learning is challenging.
- ◆ Make sure participants feel included and cared about.

19 Ways to Get Attention

◆ An introduction by someone else.

◆ Coordinate music or other fanfare.

◆ A round of applause.

◆ A strong statement about your topic.

◆ Thanking the audience in a fresh way.

◆ Eliciting curiosity with a strong probing question.

◆ A musical instrument played.

◆ Blowing a train whistle or rapping a gong.

◆ Playing a powerful video.

◆ Standing in an unusual location in the room.

◆ Using a rhythmic clap.

◆ Using a "start-up" tradition or ritual that is repeated on cue.

◆ Using physical engagement; get everyone up to applaud.

◆ Activate with novelty; an unusual costume, voice or action.

◆ Ask participants to give partner-to-partner affirmations: "Turn to the person nearest you and welcome them with a smile!"

◆ Give a fun group slogan. On cue, train everyone to say something that pulls the whole group together ("Learning is fun!").

◆ Tell a powerful metaphor that encapsulates the whole message in a few words.

◆ Play a quick game of "Simon Sez" with the audience.

◆ Share a brief, relevant story about something that's part of your topic.

To learn in a structured environment, we are often required to "pay attention" for long periods of time. The human brain has a built-in attentional bias for certain types of stimuli. Since our brain isn't designed to consciously attend to all types of incoming stimuli, it sorts out which is less critical to our survival.

14 Ways to Engage Emotions

◆ Role-model the love of learning and show enthusiasm about your job. Example: show off a new CD, book, object, clothing item, pet, etc.

◆ Celebrate. When something is accomplished, make a big deal out of it: party favors, balloons, music, let people dance or brag to others about what they accomplished

◆ Acknowledgments. Use certificates, verbal statements, team sharing or compliments.

◆ Parties can be a planned after-work activity or a fun impromptu toast.

◆ High-five's, low-fives, high-tens, etc.

◆ Let people get up, experiment and have fun!

◆ Food. Either you bring it, the audience brings it, it's catered or a combination

◆ Music. Use movie themes, TV themes, catchy pop songs, jazz, Motown, country, soul, or marches.

◆ Theater, role-play and drama. Example: Groups volunteer to put on a skit or role-play. There's rehearsals, stress, fun, anxiety, anticipation, suspense, excitement and relief.

◆ Controversy. It could be a debate, dialogue, argument, real or artificial.

◆ Rituals. Through the purposeful use of rituals, make the process fun and inter active. Example: for introductions, each learner gets three claps and a "whoosh"!

◆ Teams. Groups can create plenty of engagement and emotion. Example: each team has a special cheer for each member upon arrival.

◆ Games, activities and energizers that get everyone going like musical chairs, bingo, Simon Sez, etc.

◆ Great stories, and human drama can be used to bring relevant personal meaning to the learning.

Quickie Tips for Getting Audience Cooperation

◆ Welcome and greet arrivees by name at the front door if possible.

◆ Shake hands, be warm, genuine and smile.

◆ Be physical. Ask everyone to change seats with the person next to them.

◆ Use "loops," incomplete actions or words as cliffhangers to hold attention.

◆ Provide immediate WIIFM— "What's In It For Me? Announce benefits.

◆ Gather information: ask audience members where they're from; and where they work?

◆ Open with three key words you'd like the audience to remember and they will!

◆ Use positive body language, smile and create positive expectancy.

◆ Use an object like a picture, magazine cover, prop or instrument.

◆ Give genuine compliments; acknowledge their commitment.

◆ Be sure to reassure audience of the seminar's or training's value.

◆ Avoid giving long lists; group them into a clusters of three or four.

◆ Use an unusual action, position, or gesture that engages curiosity.

◆ Wear a crazy costume like that of a literary character, a scientist or local hero.

◆ Ask audience questions: who drove a half hour or more to get here, one hour, two?

◆ Announce hot news; can be the real thing or invented news.

◆ Offer and use a real-life problems that directly relates to the audience.

◆ Employ special visuals, such as a big posterboard sign or poster.

◆ Bring up two or three participants at a time and have them introduce themselves.

◆ Try out an unusual stage design—lighting or backdrop.

◆ Innovate with wild decorations—flowers, plants or ribbons.

14 Fun Group-Bonding Rituals

◆ Start the course each day with a rousing or inspirational song. Preferably the same song each time.

◆ Open the day with call-responses: like "Goooo-oood Morning to You!

◆ Do a "Yes" clap at the end of a 90 minute segment right before the break.

◆ High-fives after a paired activity or group pair-share.

◆ Have a short walk with a partner to share insights.

◆ Use affirmations: "Turn to the person nearest you and say, 'Great job!'"

◆ Use a real "round" of applause (hands moving in a circle while applauding) or do an audience wave (standing and sitting one row at a time in synchronization).

◆ Ask teams to do a daily self-assessment.

◆ Invent a cheer to do after participant introductions.

◆ Share jokes at the lunch break.

◆ Use the same "call-in" or music to bring participants back after a break.

◆ Stretching. Ask participants to stand up, join their team or pick a partner and face each other. Play relaxing music and do slow deep breathing to oxygenate the body.

◆ Mind-mapping can be a daily ritual. Ask the participants to get out paper and make a mind-map of yesterday's learning from memory. Allow the participants about ten minutes to talk to a person near them to refresh their memory.

◆ Review prior knowledge with another learner. Share respective mind-maps.

14 More Wild Attention-Getters

◆ Provide a live music opening or other fanfare as you're introduced.

◆ Make a particularly strong statement that evokes emotions.

◆ Have participants write their name in a special color or with their non-dominant hand.

◆ Be introduced by audio tape, or by a video.

◆ Preview entire course at high-speed using all the overheads and music.

◆ Elicit curiosity with a startling question.

◆ Use brain activators like cross-lateral movements.

◆ Give an example of your expertise that is a bit unusual.

◆ Immerse the room in powerful visuals—might be posters or peripherals.

◆ Create a special event like an auction or game show.

◆ Use unusually colored or cartoon overheads.

◆ Take advantage of special CDs or tapes of movie themes; find out what movies are "hot" and use those as attention-getters.

◆ **Solve an immediate problem faced by the audience** (getting materials, finding parking, lunch, getting name tags, units of credit, something to write with, etc.).

◆ Bring your pet—your dog, cat, snake, bird, ferret or other novelty.

Ideas for Physical Participation

1 Apprentice Time

Ask participants to write an area of expertise they have on their name tag. Have audience members pair up and take a few minutes to discuss their respective talents and knowledge.

2 Re-enactments

Students learn at the cellular level when the body is involved; for example, by enacting role-plays or simulations of real-life events. It could be role-played the "wrong" way, then re-done the "right" way to maximize the concept. Give learners time to plan the re-enactment well. Make it fun, with lots of positive feedback.

3 Games

Many childhood games are still appropriate. I've used the following with great success: musical chairs, ball toss, bingo, quiz shows and horseshoes. The secret is in how you set up the game. I have seen conservative, "case-hardened" audiences truly enjoy games that had a clear purpose and that were organized to be fun.

4 Re-grouping

There are many ways to group and re-group participants in order to encourage participation:

- ◆ Participants sit where they are, but rotate their chairs to face three others.
- ◆ Put two, three, or four chairs side to side, facing each other.
- ◆ Walk in any direction eleven steps; pair up with the nearest person.
- ◆ Stand up and walk as many steps in the room as the date of your birthday (i.e., for August 5th, walk 5 steps). Then pair up with the nearest person.
- ◆ Have participants group up with others who have common characteristics (i.e., height, clothing color, gender, hair color, etc.).

5 Voting With the Body

Ask the audience to take an action to express their interest in something. For example:

- ◆ If you're ready to continue, have a seat.
- ◆ If you'd like to learn something new, please be seated.
- ◆ If your partner had some good ideas, give them a high-five.
- ◆ If you're ready for a break, please stand up.
- ◆ If you're ready for a quick stretch, please stand up.

7 Ideas for Greater Conversational Participation

1 Case Studies

Discussions led by a qualified facilitator where scenarios from real-life experiences are used to apply learning.

2 Response Cards

The audience responds in writing on index cards to questions posed by the teacher. They may respond with answers, comments or more questions. Collect the cards and respond to the whole group after you've had a chance to review them.

3 Fishbowls

A circle within a circle is formed by your audience members with their chairs. The inner circle discusses an issue while the outer circle listens and takes notes on the group dynamics, process, or content. After the prearranged time limit is up, the outer circle gets to share their observations or ask questions. The groups then rotate, so that each of them does both aspects of the exercise.

4 Focus Sessions

In small groups, participants express their opinion on questions asked by the leader. The leader helps keep the group focused on sharing, fair treatment of group members and staying on task.

5 Jigsaw Groupings

A topic is provided and teams start by brainstorming the topic in separate circles. Then after the prearranged time limit, members from the group divide—one member goes to one group, another member goes to another group where the topic is discussed again or their list shared. Only the leader of the group remains in the same place. The members of the new groups add any new information to their notes. Then, everyone returns to their original team. Now they re-share their improved lists and refine the ideas even further.

6 Panel Discussions

Divide a group of participants based on their strong opposing opinions about a topic or subject. Then put the strongest opposite positions on a panel together with between two and five participants on each side. The rest of the participants become the audience who can ask questions and keep the panel discussions alive.

7 Polling

Ask for a vote on a topic. Your "in-house poll" could be:

◆ Verbal: yes or no; yeah or nay
◆ Written: a ballot or questionnaire
◆ Kinesthetic: hands raised; or vote by moving to this or that location in the classroom

How do you plan on encouraging your audience's participation in your next presentation?

Quick Ways to Form Partnerships

People can get too comfortable with the same partner, so mix things up a bit. To select new partners:

1 Say to the whole group, "Please stand up."

2 "Now take seven (at least 5, less than 25) steps in any direction and pause."

3 "Now, find the person who is closest to you in height."

4 "Next, find the person who is wearing the same colors as you are."

5 "Find the first person who has a birthday in your same month."

6 "Make the sound of a pet you have. Pair up with another person who has the same pet.

7 "Find the nearest person who has your hair color."

8 "Pick the nearest person you don't know."

9 "Let's play psychic—close your eyes, spin around once and point to another person. Did that same person point to you? They're your partner."

In a short training there will not be time for extended democratic processes. Therefore, when you need to form a group, you'll need to do it quickly. Simply announce your decision to the group in a quick and fun way: "The person who will (do the task, start up, etc.) will be the one who..."

10 Is wearing the most (or least) amount of jewelry.

11 Has the longest (or shortest) hair.

12 Is sitting closest to the door (or window, etc.).

13 Has the curliest hair.

14 Is wearing clothes with the most colors.

15 Is the tallest (or shortest).

16 Has the most (or least) amount of buttons.

17 Has the shiniest shoes.

18 Is wearing the most amount of white (or blue, black, etc.).

What are some activities you use to form groups or partnerships? Are there any new ideas you would like to try?

# Ways to Form Instant Groups

You may want a group to perform a task for five to twenty minutes. You may want to offer a break from the team just to prevent things from getting too stale. In either case, you need a quickly-formed group. Here are some ideas on how to do it:

1 Numbering

If your group size is under fifty, have everyone number off, from one to five (or any number from four to ten), depending on the total number in your room and what size you want each group. After each person has a number, ask all the one's to hold up one finger, two's—two fingers, etc. while everyone finds their respective groups.

2 Pets

Ask participants who have dogs to go to this side of the class; and everyone who has cats to go to that side; and anyone who has both to go to the center of the room, and those who don't have either to go to the sharing area, etc.

3 Birthdays

Ask participants to find others who have birthdays in the same month. This, of course, will give you twelve groups. If you want to divide the groups further, you can say those whose birthdays are in the first half of the month versus those in the last half of the month.

4 House Numbers

They hold up the number on their fingers of the first digit of their address (or last digit of their phone number, etc.) and find others who are holding up the same number.

5 Name

Ask participants to find their group by identifying those whose first name starts with the same letter as theirs. Name tags are suggested for this exercise.

6 Clothing

Ask participants to find people wearing the primary color they are wearing to form the group.

7 Teams

Let people choose partners based on high school, college or professional sports teams they favor.

8 Roles

Ask participants to code their name tags by letters which describe the job they have. Then let people pick others based on sameness or diversity.

9 Room Location

Ask learners to walk around the room while the music is playing. When the music stops they are to stop and go to the closest corner of the room to form four teams.

10 Hair Color

Blondes go to this corner; brunettes to that corner.

11 Preferences

If you are more like an apple than an orange, go to this side of the room. If you are more like a sports car than a truck, go to that side of the room.

Make sure you allow your group's time, either structured or unstructured to relax and play together. Let them do a skit, play a game, a sport, sing, go out to eat, etc. This allows the team a chance to lower their guard and really get to each other better. The more your team members know each other, the more they accept each other and will work together to succeed.

25 Ideas:

Sharpening Your Communications

Key Nonverbal Signals

- Arms extended outward, palms up - indicates a choice, a question or an invitation.

- Arms extended outward, palms down, crossing each other quickly and repeatedly like a baseball umpire declaring "safe" at home plate - indicates signal to the audience to stop or it means "no way."

- One hand out and palm facing forward like a traffic cop - indicates to the audience, stop and listen.

- Chopping motion or use of the edge of the hand in an up-down motion - indicates the end of something. You can also use the finger drawn from side-to-side across the throat.

- Shaking of fist(s) briefly and sparingly - indicates intensity. I use it to symbolize a victory cheer, like one that goes with the saying, "Yes!"

- Arms extended outward, palms down - indicates the desire for the audience to settle down or have a seat.

- Both arms extended straight up, high above head, like an umpire signaling a field goal - indicates a celebration.

- Numbers: If you say you're going to present three key ideas, be sure to show three fingers.

- Size: If you say something is "huge" use widely outstretched arms. If you say something is small, use thumb and forefinger held slightly apart.

- Position: If you say something is "over there," use your hands to demonstrate the distance. If you discuss two ideas, always stand in two different places to illustrate their differences.

- Persons: If you refer to yourself or another person, insure your hands either point to you or away respectively.

- Action Steps: To indicate stop, pause, start or wait for the next instruction, use the motions typically used by a traffic officer.

5 Smart Things to Do (or Not Do) With Your Hands

1 Engage one of them, let the other hang loosely
- Hold something in one hand
- Gesture with one of them
- Use a prop
- Hold a mike

2 Use both of them
- Use both hands to gesture at the same time if you have an important point.
- Avoid constantly gesturing or you'll be "crying wolf," and the audience won't respond when you do need stronger emphasis.

3 Steepling
- Hold your two hands loosely together with fingers slightly spread and fingertips touching. Hands are waist to chest high. Wrists are about 6-8" apart and tips of fingers point upwards.

4 Watch your hands
- Avoid both hands at your side for more than a few seconds or both hands in pockets.

5 Avoid fidgeting
- Avoid scratching, fidgeting, biting nails, playing with hair, grooming activities, or nervous habits on stage.

Easy Steps for Providing Effective Instructions

1. First get learners into an appropriate state. For example, say "Let's do something fun. First, take in a deep breath and stand up!" This creates a state of curiosity and anticipation.

2. Explain the reason for doing it. "How many of you played musical chairs as a kid? And how many of you still like to have fun in one form or another? How about if we mix learning with having fun!"

3. State when the "fun" starts. For example, say "In just a moment, we will..."

4. Specifically address those being asked to take action. For example, "Everyone..." or "Those of you in group one..."

5. State the specific course of action to be taken. For example, "Move your chair to form a big oval, like the shape of a racetrack. Then wait for further instruction."

6. Clarify, or restate directions in another way. For example, "This means the chairs will be right next to each other, facing each other in a big, elongated circle or oval.

7. Ask for questions and feedback. For example, "Before we start this session, who wants clarification?"

8. Make sure there is a congruent call to action. For example, "Ready?... get set... go!" (Keep this call to action the same each time.)

66 Ideas:

Quickie
Energizers &
State Changers

Secrets for Creating an Energized Audience

1 Energizers are generally used to change the state of the participants. Remind them that the mind and body work together. If the body's tired and lifeless, the mind needs waking up, too. Make direct links (if they exist) to the learning. People will do all kinds of fun, silly or even bizarre activities if there's a good reason for it.

2 Plan, plan, plan. Think every activity all the way through. Plan for:
- ◆ How much room you'll need.
- ◆ How to do the pairings and groupings.
- ◆ What to do with tables or chairs.
- ◆ What music selections you'll use.
- ◆ The props, supplies and materials needed.
- ◆ Clear directions for each step; post them.
- ◆ How to get everyone involved.
- ◆ What to do if part of the energizer fails.
- ◆ How to make the activity relevant.
- ◆ Timing and length of energizer.
- ◆ The debriefing and follow up.

3 Make the activities non-threatening. In a game like musical chairs, make sure that everyone has already brainstormed some possible responses *before* the game begins. In other activities, allow participants the right to "pass" and let the game rotate to the next person. Low to moderate stress is entirely appropriate to the brain in learning. Strong threat is not.

4 Keep the activities short. While there are many exceptions, in general, it's better to have an activity too short than too long. Make sure that learners get the point of the activity and that it was developed sufficiently. But at the same time, you want to prevent boredom, too.

5

Novelty is powerful. If you're going to use a game over again, give it a twist. If a game is going to go on for a while, let participants get involved in making the rules. Change the props, the groupings or the content to prevent things from getting stale.

6

Keep it fun. As soon as a game becomes too stressful or too focused on content, the game's over. Participants ought to be able to be engaged, relaxed and enjoy themselves in the process.

7

Fun and content *can* go together. Musical chairs, for example, can become a review game if the person left standing shares one or two ideas that he or she has learned from the previous day. In fact, every single energizer can also become a learning activity if you use some creativity to give it a content twist.

> ***What energizing activity is planned into your next presentation?***

50 State Change Suggestions

- Change Where You Stand in the Room
- Post Affirmations
- Wear Special Hats/Clothes
- Make Faces
- Expressions
- Special Gestures
- Use Videos/Overhead Projector
- Mime
- Stand on Chair or Table
- Point to Something
- Do a Visualization
- Stand Still
- Mind-Map Material
- Turn Your Back on the Group
- Hold Up an Object
- Change Lighting
- Do a Magic Trick
- Leave the Room
- Conduct a Stretch Break
- Ball Toss/Footbag/Pillow
- Drink Water
- Change Seats
- Do Cross Lateral Activities
- Role Play/Theater
- Play Games, Hands-on Learning
- Read With Passion (out loud)
- Laugh/Tell a Joke
- Sing/Use Whistles
- Group and Team Work
- Change Tonality
- Oral Affirmations
- Use Music
- Tell a Story/Metaphor
- Ask Questions
- Partner Re-Present
- Discussions/Debates
- Participants Present
- Repeat What Was Just Said
- Scream, Pause, Silence
- Use Sound Effect
- Knock on Door
- Use Several Names
- Repeat After Me
- Potpourri
- Food
- Flowers
- Popcorn/Fresh Bread
- Take a Deep Breath
- Stomp Feet
- Sub-Divide Groups

The amount of stimulation that the human brain can accept and integrate is astonishing. The sounds of your room are just as important as the looks and feel of it. While your room may be visually attractive, 40% of your learners will learn best by sounds.

Active Stretch Break Ideas

1 Drama

Conduct pantomimes of recent learning in teams or dyads.

2 Simon Sez

Conduct a well-known game that gets everyone participating.

3 Pair and Share

"What have I learned" exchange (with a partner) while standing and stretching.

4 Oxygen

In small groups, have a leader facilitate breathing and stretching relaxers.

5 Walk and Learn

Take a "walking review" with a partner for five minutes.

6 Something New

Take the group outside for a change of location learning break.

7 Cross-Lateral Stimulators

These include patting yourself on one side of your back with the opposite hand, touching opposite elbows, opposite hips, opposite heels, etc.

8 Creative Handshakes

Everyone stands up and introduces themselves three others, each time inventing a new way to shake the new person's hand. This builds creativity. Variations include three ways to say hello, three ways to say good-bye, etc.

9 Poster Parade

Stand up and find a partner. Look around the room and visually pick out two or three posters that you like. Take your partner with you, walk over to the posters and tell your partner why they are meaningful for you.

54 Ideas:

Learning Transfer

16 Ways to Insure Participants Remember

◆ Ask teams to sequence or organize information or key ideas written on cards.

◆ Combine intense visual images (photographs, slides, posters, video, etc.) with spoken and printed words.

◆ Go multi-media. Make your presentation as visual, auditory and kinesthetic as possible.

◆ Learn through a rap song. The best one is the one that the audience makes up.

◆ Pre-expose participants to content to be learned in advance; then post it during active learning phase; and review it one week (1 day, or hours) later.

◆ Post key ideas on poster board or have learners make story boards.

◆ Have participants become presenters.

◆ Use flash cards for review. Make a game out of it.

◆ Use role-play to engage the learning. The time participants spend planning is as important as the actual performance.

◆ Ask audience to prepare a list of the ten most important questions answered in the presentation.

◆ Have learning teams generate two-minute commercials to present to the others.

◆ Encourage study groups that meet at lunch or other times when the training is not in session.

◆ Learn through chanting. Different than a rap, a chant might be like a military march (i.e., "1,2,3,4... I know lots, so give me more").

◆ Give everyone colored highlighter pens. Ask them to review their workbooks using them with a color- coding system that prioritizes information.

◆ Ask participants to work in small groups to evaluate key ideas presented in your workshop by putting cards (with ideas on them) into categories like "Wow" for good ideas, "OOPS" for uncertainties and "Ho-Hum" for boring or useless ideas. Then, have them share their groupings and rationale with the whole group.

◆ Present information in chunks of seven or fewer items. No matter how much you have to say, break it into chunks of seven for ease in recall.

 Though we now know how critical meaning is to the learning process, most learners are drowning in information and starved for meaning.

Strategies for Long-Term Retention

◆ Have an unguided group discussion on the material, it's value, and what was or was not learned.

◆ Relate the content to something similar through metaphors, then share that discovery with others.

◆ Make the learning out of the ordinary, unusual, bizarre, humorous, sexy, or personal.

◆ Use an unusual voice to signal the subject's importance.

◆ Attach a strong positive or negative feeling to the material.

◆ Provide a concrete reminder like a token, trophy, certificate, toy or artifact.

◆ Create a silly story to recall the information.

◆ Use memory peg systems. For example, link key information with an object or number.

◆ Write things down that are critical so that you can focus on other things. This allows your mind to stay "present" to the matters at hand.

◆ Believe in yourself. Having confidence lowers your stress.

◆ Avoid negative self-talk and worry.

◆ Encourage learners to eat good foods for memory like lecithin supplements (or wheat germ and egg yolks).

◆ Use a prop, especially a bizarre one to reinforce the learning.

◆ Make the material into an instructional book or comic book.

◆ Make a poster, collage or graffiti.

◆ Creates something novel or fun (i.e., a T-shirt) to recall information.

◆ The more you review and the more recently you review, the better you'll remember.

◆ Use the BEM principle (beginning, end and middle): use lots of beginnings and endings.

◆ Be sure to review after ten minutes, forty-eight hours and seven days.

◆ Use the future pace; phrases like, "When you remember this...."

◆ Unfinished tasks are recalled better than completed ones; leave some undone on purpose.

◆ Use acronyms: key words where the first letter stands for an idea to be remembered.

◆ Relate the material to a larger picture.

◆ Have learners tell an embellished story about the material.

14 Ideas That Nearly Guarantee Transfer of Learning

◆ **Make the learning so valuable that learners almost have to use it.**

◆ **Create better buy-in from the start. Encourage learner's input.**

◆ **Use multiple practice trials to reinforce comfort level.**

◆ **Provide condition-action rules so that learners know when to use what ideas or strategies and how.**

◆ **Evoke strong meaning with participants through emotions and relevance.**

◆ **Provide a variety of visual tools and mapping activities so participants can find all the connections.**

◆ **Build on the participant's motivation to learn, whatever it is** (i.e., school credit, pay raise, networking).

◆ **Increase accountability. Check in with learners, observe groups, design "score-keeping" devices, have groups present back to the group, etc.**

◆ **Use metaphors - either one that you construct or simply adapt others that are commonly used** (even childhood fables can be re-worked).

◆ **Remove potential barriers - find out what keeps participants from implementing change; it might be embarrassment, fear, or lack of know how.**

◆ **Apply structural analogies and put learning in context so participants can make associations and meaning from previous learning.**

◆ **Capitalize on the non-conscious learning process** (i.e., through peripherals, affirmations, music, etc.).

◆ **Make change an easy proposition - set up a simple, fast, first step.**

◆ **Support learning in real-life contexts - discuss how learning applies back at the office or wherever.**

67 Ideas: Combining Fun With Learning

13 Tips for Better Activities

1. Keep the activity short and well focused.

2. Make the activity meaningful; explain why you're doing it.

3. Give clear directions; rehearse them in your mind first.

4. Change the type of activities to keep them fresh.

5. Make sure that you're enthusiastic about the activity.

6. Make sure the activity is relevant to the learning.

7. Be sure to keep track the results.

8. Create smooth transitions from one step to the next.

9. Prepare all overheads and flip charts in advance.

10. Give crisp, clear, easy-to-understand directions.

11. Create a system for getting volunteers; never wait - just jump in.

12. Use time deadlines; and stick to them.

13. Use music as a backdrop for the activity.

6 Highly Effective Activity Signals

1 Use a consistent verbal message. Instead of the phrase, "Stop and listen up," I like to use, "Pause please" This is a bit softer and more inviting.

2 Use a clapping signal. Either a triple clap or begin a clap-respond ritual.

3 Turn lights on or off quickly a couple of times or dim the lights.

4 Use a sound effect on tape (i.e., a police siren, a church bell, or gong).

5 Whistles; the small plastic tooter whistles are better than a coach's whistle which might be too piercing.

6 Use a silent sign which might be as simple as a hand raised, a jingle bell, or a sign that says, "Your silence is requested, please."

What other ideas do you have for signals? With what age groups are they most important?

Limited Space Activities

1 Cross-Laterals

The purpose of these are to activate and energize the brain through movement. Especially useful are cross-laterals or cross-overs where you touch the opposite side of your body with one hand or foot - right to left or left to right. Touch hands to opposite knees, give yourself a pat on the back on opposite sides, touch opposite heels, air swimming - one arm moving in one direction the other arm moving in the other, touch nose and hold opposite ear then switch, do "lazy 8s" in front of you by tracing the pattern of the number eight with your hand in the thumb up sign. Start your 8 at the center, arms length, going up and to the right, do big loops on both sides and switch sides.

2 Frisbee Review

Throw a Frisbee to someone. Whoever catches the Frisbee, states one thing that they've learned in the last couple of minutes or hours. It gets more exciting the more Frisbees you have going at once. Other objects can be used like a Koosh ball or Nerf ball, as well.

3 Matching Faces-Matching Sounds

With the group standing in a large circle, a volunteer starts by making a weird face or sound which is then "passed" on to the person next to them in the circle. Then, this person passes it on to the person next to them, until it's gone all the way around the circle, at which time a new person starts up the cycle. Variations are to pass a face in one direction and a sound in the other or pass a "body movement."

4 New Seats

Everybody stands and switches seats. The new seat must be at least ten feet away from the old one. Put on music during the transition and do this whenever things get stale or the audience needs a little break.

5 Simon Sez

Everyone stands and does only what Simon (you) says to do. Give instructions to follow, some of them prefaced with "Simon says," and others simply given alone. Go at a moderate pace. If mistakes are made, keep playing. Always make it a win for all, so no one's ever out of the game.

6 Toybox

Keep a box of toys in your training room for break time. They might include a paddle ball, tennis balls, a Frisbee, a Koosh, inflatables, Hula Hoops, hats, stress-reducers, models, Playdough, noisemakers, puppets, a football and other kid's toys. These relieve stress and make for a more playful training.

7 Writing Your Name

Participants stand up and write their first name with their elbow, their middle name with their other elbow, their last name with their hip, their best friend's name with their other hip and their mom's or dad's name with their head. You can easily add course content. Using your head, write the most important key concept from the last hour. Use your leg to write out the most important key concept from yesterday. Get partners to form a chorus line and do several words from last week.

How do you plan on incorporating learning activities into your presentation?

7 Open Space Activities

1 Ad-Ons

Use as an icebreaker or for review. Invite one person to come up to the front of the room. They pose in a posture or movement from something that they have learned from the course. Another comes up and joins the impromptu living sculpture, adding on people until a giant human scenario is made that represents what they've been learning. The final product might be a machine, a system changing, an example of superior customer service or a human brain.

2 Ball Toss

Great for forming teams. Can be used to introduce others or for review. 5-7 participants stand in a circle about 10 feet apart, facing each other. One has a ball or bean bag. He tosses it to a person to start the game. Content could be "Q & A," or continuing a story, giving a compliment, word association, facts, review, etc. Keep the game fast and light. Give participants control and clear set rules. Ball Toss Variations: Use a Koosh, a soft Frisbee, a water balloon, or other novel item. Use it as a review, brainstorm, introduction or self-disclosure tool.

3 Lap Sit

A great icebreaker or closure activity. All participants stand in a circle, facing the back of the person in front of them. Each person holds on to the waist of the person in front of them; and on cue, everyone sits down simultaneously on the person's lap behind them!

4 Role-Plays

Either as a large or small group, it's like quick theater. You might give your participants an idea and let them fill in it. They might get a detailed script from you and fill it in. They can re-enact a real-life situation that recently occurred.

5 Touch and Go

Get up, in sequence, touch five pieces of gold, four pieces of silver, three of glass, two of leather, and one clothing label on someone else. All items must be at least ten feet apart. Variations on the game above: instead of touching those items, make the game part of the content you are presenting.

6 Triangle Tag

Triangle tag requires a group of four. Three people form a triangle, holding hands; the fourth stands outside the group and tries to tag whoever is "it." The triangle team keeps spinning to avoid having the "it" person tagged!

7 Tug of War

Everyone gets a partner and picks a topic from the list of things learned. Each person has their own topic and their goal is to convince their partner in an argument why their topic is more important. After the verbal discussion, settle it physically with a giant tug of war. Take the group outside. All partners should be on opposite sides. Settle the "dispute."

Scientists have gathered data that supports the mind-body connection. These studies have examined the role that enrichment, nutrition, exercise, lifestyle, and feelings play in learning. How will these variables get accounted for in your next presentation?

6 Discussion Activities

1 Brain Transplants

On index cards or Post-It notes, ask participants to write a talent, experience or belief about themselves. For example, a person might write "surfing" on one piece and "traveled to Africa" on another. Have participants attach them to their clothing (up high) and let people mingle for a few minutes. You are to make at least one trade with another person, and you can make up to three trades. Afterwards, let people share what and why they made the trades that they did.

2 Case Studies

Great for teams to review or learn new material. A team is either given a written history of an actual event or watches a video of it. The team's job is to study the events, discuss what happened, how it happened and guess the outcome. What occurred? What could have been done differently? How and why? Make a presentation on it, do a debate or write a summary and present it.

3 Expert Interviews

Divide the audience in half. One half becomes the "experts" in the topic you're presenting; the other half the famous "reporters." The reporters proceed to interview the experts for two minutes to "get the story." Then reverse the roles.

4 Humor

At the outset of the course, ask for volunteers who know a joke and would be willing to share it. All volunteers put their name on the flip chart and at any point during the day, a participant can call on them to tell their joke. It's a good break.

5 Hot Seat

A great closing activity. Each team sits in a circle. One person is "it." Everyone gets sixty seconds to say acknowledgments to the person in the hot seat. The listener has to remain silent or say only "Thank you." Rotate the next person into the hot seat.

6 Laughter

Use team joke-telling for a break or state change. Each team gets three minutes to share their favorite jokes among themselves. Then each team votes on their favorite joke and asks that person if they would be willing to share it with the big group.

Extra-Loud Activities

1 Barnyard

Use as an icebreaker or a fun way to form groups. Assign a number to everyone, up to the number of groups you want (i.e., if six groups, everyone gets a number from one to six). Or, if you want six groups, simply go by birthday months. Assign a noisy animal from the barnyard to all groups. For example the ones are all dogs, the twos are all cats, all threes are sheep, all fours are goats, all fives are chickens and all sixes are horses. Then, have all of them stand up, and mix for thirty seconds. Then ask participants to close their eyes and make their respective animal sounds. Groups are formed as participants find like animals by sound. This can be a riot of fun! With more conservative groups, allow them to keep their eyes open.

2 Childhood Song Redo

Ask each group to pick a favorite song. Suggestions include: She'll Be Coming Around the Mountain, Rover, Red Rover, Row, Row, Row Your Boat, Happy Birthday, Old MacDonald, etc. The teams then replace key words from the songs with the key words from the learning, add choreography, and perform it.

3 Clapping Games

Use as an energizer and a way to align the group. You start a clap or rhythm, and participants pass it around the room. Then the first participant starts a clapping rhythm and others follow suit. Good for memory and music skills.

4 Holding the Bag

This is the same concept as musical chairs except you don't use chairs. To start the game, you ask everyone to stand up and walk around the room giving positive affirmations to other participants, while playing fun, loud music. Give a bean bag to someone who passes it to another and says, "You're now holding the bag, but you're a genius." The receiver has to say, "I know I'm a genius, but I'm now stuck holding the bag." When the music stops, the one holding the bag (or ball or whatever) shares with the group one thing they learned from the day's lessons.

5 Musical Chairs

First, individuals, pairs, or teams, brainstorm a topic. This gives everyone something to talk about later. Then ask the audience to mill around and talk or dance. When the music stops, everyone grabs a chair. The one left standing, shares with the group one thing they learned from the day's lessons.

Physically Charged Team Activities

1 Charades

Charades is a perfect physical activity for reviewing material. Give each team of three to five a range of topics and a deadline to design a non-verbal "commercial" on their topic of choice. Provide visuals. When ready, each team presents their charade to the big group.

2 Follow the Leader

Follow the Leader can be used as a review, a memory game, perception practice, or skills practice. A team or group leader acts out the learning, others follow along and repeat.

3 Gordian Knot

Good for building teamwork. Teams of six or eight stand in a circle, facing each other approximately two feet apart. One participant reaches out with one hand and clasps the hand of the person directly across from them. Each person clasps the hand of the opposite person, until everyone is holding hands. Now, the group must untie themselves from the giant knot without releasing hands.

4 Simulations

Good for learning about group dynamics. Simulation activities ask individuals or groups to read about a situation and make decisions about it. While it's rarely able to match the real thing, it does provide some terrific opportunities for problem-solving, creativity, teamwork and planning. Some of the best simulation games are the "survival games" like simulated Arctic survival, jungle survival, desert survival and mountain survival.

5 Team Massage

Best as a wake-up energizer. Use for age appropriate groups only. Everyone stands up with their left shoulders facing the center of the circle. Put on music. Each person massages the shoulders of the person standing in front of them.

Team Affirmations

Put this list up on an overhead or pass out duplicated copies of it. Ask the team leader to read it aloud with energy and enthusiasm; or rotate around the group having each participant read an affirmation. At the end, do a cheer.

◆ **I'm glad you're on my team.**

◆ **Learning is easy on this team.**

◆ **You make it all happen!**

◆ **Anything is possible on our team.**

◆ **Terrific teamwork!**

◆ **This team is getting better every day.**

◆ **Number one and getting higher!**

◆ **Together team achieves more.**

◆ **This is what I call amazing!**

◆ **Together we can make miracles.**

◆ **Perfect ten out of ten!**

◆ **Each of us is unique and valuable.**

◆ **I'm impressed!**

◆ **Our team spirit is sky high.**

◆ **Yes-team! Yes-team...Yes!**

◆ **We are the team of destiny.**

◆ **I know we'll succeed!**

◆ **This is the best team ever!**

Our world is full of affirmations. We say "Have a great day," or "Happy Holidays," or "Be careful." Why do we affirm? We like to wish the best for others. Affirmations "make firm" that which you want. It's a suggestion, a prediction, a blessing and well-wishing. The more you affirm goodness in others, the likely you are to find goodness.

50 Ideas:
Closing Your Presentation

8 Keys to Perfect Closings

1 Elicit a Feeling of Movement

Your audience needs to know how far they have come in their learning.

2 Insure Meaning

Your audience needs to apply the learning to their own lives.

3 Establish Value

Your audience needs to know how the learning is important.

4 Elicit Wholeness

Your audience needs to understand how the key pieces fit together.

5 Provide Next Steps

Your audience needs to know what they can do to continue learning the subject.

6 Eliminate Barriers to Action

Your audience needs to know how to overcome the obstacles and challenges.

7 Embed Stakes in the Outcome

Your audience will be more inclined to learn if the cost-benefit ratio is high; that is, if the benefits for learning are high and the costs for not learning are high.

8 Future Pacing

Your audience needs to have a clear image of how things can turn out.

14 Ways to Elicit a Feeling of Movement

◆ Brainstorm what was learned with a team, group, or partner.

◆ Provide about five minutes of reflection time, then have participants share insights with a partner.

◆ Provide a review set to music listened to with eyes closed.

◆ Use a chart or rubric for teams to track their own progress. Go over the charts at the end of the training.

◆ Participants receive a thermometer diagram labeled "most confident" at the top and "least confident" at the bottom of the thermometer. As the course progresses, participants take stock of their understanding of the material and color in the thermometer accordingly.

◆ Each team creates three or four key crossword questions and answers related to the learning. Then they are combined with the other groups questions to create a large class crossword puzzle.

◆ In a peer teaching format, present what you've learned to another person.

◆ Play musical chairs and the one left standing shares one course idea that was valuable to them.

◆ Participants fill in the blanks, in unison, to your verbal review questions.

◆ Play a word association game where everyone gets a list of ten wild words to link up with ten key ideas from the course.

◆ Utilize a test or other form of assessment.

◆ Have participants use a learning log or diary, then share it with a partner.

◆ Participants check their learning against a list of goals they set (or you set) at the beginning of the training.

◆ Teams brainstorm key ideas, then use memory review principles to memorize them, and share their strategies with the larger group.

Strategies to Insure Meaning and Value

- Mesh the learning into a larger pattern of understanding. This can be accomplished, in part, through mind maps and small group discussions.

- Have participants make personal audio tapes of their learning. On the final day of the session supply everyone with tapes and set up recording stations around the room. Participants can record a tape of the top ten things they learned for later listening and review.

- Elicit from participants conclusions they have drawn from the day's learning and its relevancy to their lives.

- Trigger meaningful or powerful emotions. This can be done with personal experiences, music, competition, drama, case studies, team rituals or celebrations.

- Do a performance for an outside group that incorporates the learning.

- Have partners or teams do a rating chart or rubric with each other.

- Drop a handful of overheads or cue cards with key ideas on them and ask the group to recall the order the information was learned as you attempt to reorganize the cue cards. This activity can also be done in small groups.

- Have learners list what they have learned and select ideas that they want to implement.

- Have teams demonstrate a new skill from the learning.

- Listen to others share what they learned in the training. Everyone contributes.

- Pass out questions to half the group and answers to the other half on cards or half pages. Then everyone looks for their matching half.

- Have participants write a letter to themselves regarding what they learned, how it applies to their life and how they anticipate implementing what they learned. Mail the letters back to participants in six months.

- One month after the training, ask participants for a letter or note sharing how they've used the material from the course. Then, publish the letters in an inspiring newsletter for all to read.

15 Tips to Elicit a Feeling of Completion

◆ Use a closing ritual (i.e., a song, clap, movement, etc.).

◆ Ask participants to trace their steps for the day with a partner.

◆ Use celebration, certificates, and handshakes.

◆ Complete a mind map, either individual or group.

◆ Tell a story of the group's journey for the course.

◆ Provide final question and answer time.

◆ Pass out ballots for group to nominate roles for participants like "best laugh", "wildest dresser", "most fun", "biggest volunteer", "most likely to use the materials", etc. Then hold an awards ceremony.

◆ Have individuals or teams present final projects or reports to the group.

◆ Have participants complete evaluations of the class and presenter.

◆ Have a guest speaker come in and talk about the next step for learners.

◆ Learners brainstorm what to do next, including how to deal with obstacles.

◆ Provide follow-up suggestions and resources.

◆ Handle participant's needs (lost items/transportation, messages, phone numbers, etc.).

◆ Help participants set up networks; make copies of class roster which provides phone numbers.

◆ Have a party; celebrate the learning.

37 Ideas:
Trainer's
Goodie-Bag

Cases When You Should Turn Down Work

If you want to be the best at what you do (or even be pretty good), you've got to know your limitations. A deluded self-concept or over-hyped ego ("I can do anything!") will do you much more harm than good. Never accept a work offer if:

1 You lack the time to prepare for it effectively.

2 You lack the expertise to do a good job.

3 If the sponsors are flaky or unethical.

4 If you are not happy with the compensation.

5 If the work conditions will prevent you from doing a good job.

6 If it's for the wrong audience.

7 If it will take you away from something else more important.

> *Develop your vision. You will only be as powerful in life as that which you speak about and are willing to be responsible for. What is your vision?*

Tips for Deciding How Much to Charge

1 Speaking fees for someone who is not a veteran presenter range from $250 to $1,000 per day; or $150 to $750 per half day. This "starter" compensation range is appropriate for someone who has good information and solid presentation skills, but their overall package is still a bit raw.

2 Speaking fees for someone who has a strong message, good presentation skills, excellent materials, and a name in the community or area of your specialty range from $1,000 to $2,000 per day. It is in this "shirt-sleeves" range that most presenters fall.

3 The next range is known as the "top dog" range. These are the career freelance trainers and presenters who have all the work they want. Fees range from $2,000 to $7,500 per day. They demand these high honorariums because they can get them. They represent the best in their field; they are household names to their peers.

4 Speaking fees for presenters who have a specialty niche that is rare command between $5,000 and $25,000 per day. This category of presenters, referred to as "specialists," don't necessarily have the best presenting skills, but people do want to hear them. They include celebrities, authors, professional athletes, top scientists (Nobel laureates), media personalities, Olympians, and business CEOs.

5 The "skybox" range is for the superstars. Here speaking fees range from $20,000-$100,000 per talk. They are a known, not just to the training industry, but to the general public. They include household names like ex-presidents, Colin Powell, Pat Riley, Bill Gates, Lee Iococca, Zig Ziglar, Anthony Robbins and Norman Schwartzcof.

6 To determine what category you fit into, start a bit lower than you think you can command. If you are getting too much work, your fees might be too low. Not enough work tells you either that: 1) your marketing might be weak; 2) your reputation might be too weak; 3) the competition may be strong; 4) your fees might be too high; or 5) your work quality is weak.

7 In closing, make sure that your fees are never a match for your presentation; rather make your presentation of greater value. Always deliver more than you charge and your demand will be high.

Best Trainer Books and Conferences

Best Books to Read:

◆ *Sizzle and Substance*, by Eric Jensen, The Brain Store, Inc., San Diego, CA (800) 325-4769

◆ *101 Ways to Make Training More Active*, by Mel Silberman, Pfeiffer & Co., San Diego, CA.

◆ *Secrets of Successful Speakers*, by Lilly Walters, McGraw-Hill, NY. Chock full of terrific ideas!

◆ *The Creative Trainer*, by Michael Lawlor and Peter Handley.

◆ *Active Learning*, by Mel Silberman, Pfeiffer & Co. San Diego, CA.

◆ *Tune Your Brain*, by Elizabeth Miles, Berkeley Books, NY. Great for music ideas!

◆ *Creative Training Techniques Handbook*, by Bob Pike, Lakewood Books, Minneapolis, MN, (612) 828-1960 or fax (612) 829-0260.

◆ *Inspire Any Audience*, by Tony Jeary, High Performance Resources, Dallas TX, (800) 678-8014.

◆ *Present Yourself*, by Michael Gelb, Jalmar Press, Los Angeles, CA.

Best Conferences to Attend:

◆ *Rich Allen's 5-Day Facilitator Training:* This program embodies all the critical principles of this book. Call: (888) 63-TRAIN or fax: (619) 642-0404.

◆ *International Society for Performance Improvement:* This is an excellent annual Conference. Call: (202) 408-7969 or fax: (202) 408-7972.

◆ *Eric Jensen's 6-day Training, "How the Brain Learns":* A training on how the brain learns best. Presents cutting-edge strategies in learning, plus, top guest speakers. The author's conference. Call: (888) 63-TRAIN.

◆ *ASTD:* American Society for Training and Development Annual Conference Call: (703) 683-8131.

Best Trainer Resources for Body and Brain

◆ Brain-Mind Nutritional Supplements: Smart products, herbs, vitamins, amino acids, nutritional oils, Nutrition Plus: (800) 241-9236.

◆ Life Enhancement (Brain nutrients) newsletter; for-supplements call: (800) 543-3873. They have a monthly newsletter and terrific mind-brain products.

◆ The Brain Store, Inc. The best source for trainer materials related to the brain and learning. Call: (800) 325-4769. A FREE publication.

◆ Sharing Ideas Newsletter, contact: Dottie Walters, Free sample issue. Call: (818) 335-8069.

◆ CTI (Creative Training Institute) Newsletter and Catalog, subscribe by calling: (612) 828-1960 or fax: (612) 829-0260.

◆ Creative Training Techniques Annual Program: (612) 829-1954 or fax (612) 829-0260

◆ Brain Waves Newsletter, contact: Brain Waves Editor, Minuteman Science Technology High School, 758 Marrett Rd. Lexington, MA 02173 ($3/3 issues/yr.)

◆ Consortium for Whole Brain Learning Newsletter, contact: Launa Ellison, fax: (612) 627-2376, or send correspondence: 1058 Cedar View Drive, Minneapolis, MN 55405-2129. About $15/yr.

◆ Tool Thyme for Trainers, cool training aids. Call: (504) 887-5558, ask for catalog.

◆ Wall Poster Materials, paper or plastic posters (Static Images); Staples, call: (800) 421-1222 and ask for product #618-24391.

◆ Megabrain: Tools for Exploration (Software for the Mind) Brain-mind electronic devices for state management. Call: (415) 499-9050 or fax: (415) 499-9047.

The Author

Eric Jensen is an international presenter who has taught school at all levels, trained trainers for major corporations and spoken at countless conferences. Jensen's passion is the brain and learning and is a member of the Society of Neuroscience. He remains deeply committed to making a positive, significant, lasting difference in the way the world learns. He has taught as adjunct faculty at the University of California at San Diego, National University and the University of San Diego. He's listed in "Who's Who" and is a former Outstanding Young Man of America selection.

Jensen was the co-founder of SuperCamp, the nation's first and largest brain-compatible learning program for teens. He authored the best-selling *Student Success Secrets*, *Brain-Based Learning*, *The Little Book of Big Motivation*, *Bs and As in 30 Days*, *The Learning Brain*, *Completing the Puzzle* and *Sizzle and Substance*.

He has been a key participant in brain-compatible training programs around the world. Trainers from AT & T, Disney, Motorola, BMW, Digital, Polaroid, GTE, Hewlett-Packard, CIA, Burroughs, Atlantic Bell, SAS and three branches of the military have used his methods. Jensen provides trainings for conferences, workplaces, organizations, and Fortune 500 corporations, and is an international speaker, writer and consultant.

Author Contact: Phone (619) 642-0400 or fax (619) 642-0404
Box 2551, Del Mar, California 92014 USA
E-mail: <jlcbrain@connectnet.com>
Author's WEBsite: www.jlcbrain.com

Overseas Inquiries Welcome: If you are a publisher in U.K., France, Germany, Spain, Mexico, Canada, Asia, Australia, or elsewhere, please contact our office.

Distributor Inquiries Welcome: If you distribute a catalog or do trainings, your audience may be interested in learning more about these skills and strategies. To provide catalogs and earn additional income, contact our publishing office for a distributor price list.

Notes, Thoughts and Reader's Feedback

All feedback, positive or not, is welcomed. If you have any comments, corrections, additions or suggestions for the next printing of this book, please contact the author at the address provided on the previous page. Thank you very much.

Notes

Notes

Notes